DECKS

How to

Real People – Real Projects™

HOMETIME®

Publisher: Dean Johnson
Editor: Pamela S. Price
Writer: John Kelsey
Photo Editor: Jason Adair
Copy Editor: Lisa Wagner

Hometime Hosts: Dean Johnson, Robin Hartl
Project Producers: Matt Dolph, Wade Barry
Construction and Technical Review: Chris Balamut, Dean Doying, Mark Kimball, Dan Laabs, Judd Nelson

Illustrator: Mario Ferro
Photographer: Jeff Lyman
Cover Photo: Maki Strunc Photography
Video Frame Capture: Jennifer Parks
Photoshop Effects: Steve Burmeister

Production Coordinator: Pam Scheunemann
Electronic Layout: Chris Long

Book Creative Direction, Design, and Production: MacLean & Tuminelly, Minneapolis, MN
Cover Design: Richard Scales Advertising Associates

Library of Congress Catalog Card Number 97-78174
ISBN 1-890257-04-4

HOMETIME®
4275 Norex Drive
Chaska, MN 55318

Special Thanks: Pamela Allsebrook, California Redwood Association; Chemical Specialties, Inc.; Pat Ready, Decks Unlimited; EZ-Deck; Huck DeVenzio, Hickson Corporation; Merlin's Rental Center; Richard Chapman, Simpson Strong-Tie Company, Inc.; Trex

Contributing Photography: California Redwood Association, Trex, Wolmanized® Wood, *Multi-Level Deck Design:* CaddCon Designs, Inc.

The work and procedures shown and described in this book are intended for use by people having average skills and knowledge of the subjects. If you are inexperienced in using any of the tools, equipment or procedures depicted or described, or think that the work and procedures shown and described in this book may not be safe in your chosen situation, consult a person skilled in the performance of the work or procedure. Throughout this book there are specific safety recommendations. Pay careful attention to each of these.

The makers of this book disclaim any liability for injury or damage arising out of any failure or omission to perform the work or procedures shown and described in this book. Your performance is at your own risk.

5 4 3 2 1   02 01 00 99 98

Electronic Prepress: Encore Color Group
Photo CD Scans: Procolor
Printed by: Quebecor Printing

Printed in the United States

For online project help and information on other Hometime products, visit us on the Web at **www.hometime.com**

Introduction

The time has come to take down the 2x6 that's been tacked across the sliding glass doors ever since the house was built. Or maybe it's time to tear down that shaky structure the previous owner called a deck and put up something worthy of a holiday barbecue. Either way, we know you can do it. Deck construction is pretty straightforward stuff. The tricky part is in the planning.

First off, you have to know exactly how you want to use the space. Too many people throw together decks that don't really serve their needs. In this book, we help you plan a deck that will meet your needs while accommodating your landscape, views, weather patterns, and traffic flow. In addition, we provide ideas that will help you design something that's a little more interesting than the basic rectangular deck.

Second, design a safe deck. Pay attention to the structural requirements outlined here, and spend some time talking with your local building officials. A deck that sways and bounces isn't worth the time and money you spend on it. When in doubt, overbuild.

We always enjoy building decks. You get to work outdoors and, because they go up quickly, you can see you've made good progress at the end of every day. Plus, building a deck is one of the few home improvements you can do that doesn't require you to live in a dust-covered war zone while you do it. Work safely, have fun, and remember to invite us to the barbecue.

Robin Hartl

Dean Johnson

Table of Contents

DESIGN

A simple deck costs less and is easier to build than an indoor room, yet offers three-season living space and visual appeal. With the right location and landscaping, and by adding handsome railings and stairs, and perhaps a built-in planter or bench, even a simple deck can become your yard's focal point. Large multi-level decks expand your indoor living space into a series of outdoor rooms for a variety of different activities. As with all decks, your investment will be paid back in the enjoyment you add to your lifestyle and the value you add to your home.

Assessing Your Needs

All decks serve a variety of purposes. They're used for sunning, entertaining, dining, cooking, playing, gardening, and storage. Still, you need to establish priorities to make sure your deck delivers exactly what you want in terms of size, shape, style, and function.

To start, make a wish list. Gather information from books, magazines, and home centers. Design options are limited only by your imagination and your budget, but remember that your plans will have to meet the specifications of your local building code before you begin to build.

Once you've stockpiled the ideas that appeal to you, begin to get more specific. Do this by analyzing your family's lifestyle. Do you entertain frequently? Families who routinely host large parties will have different requirements from those who prefer small, intimate gatherings. Perhaps your plan should include a pass-through window from the kitchen, or a spa or hot tub.

Outdoor entertaining *is more fun when the grill is conveniently located and out of the traffic path. You can even build an outdoor kitchen complete with cabinets and tile counters.*

A spa needs more privacy than a party deck, plus good sun and shelter from the wind. It's easiest to plan the installation of a spa before you build a deck, but you can also retrofit a spa into an existing deck.

Are you most interested in providing a play space for young children? Think about incorporating a sandbox or wading pool, and a latched gate.

Locating the deck where it's visible from one or more windows or doors helps bring the outdoors inside. The large, flat surface of a deck can easily take the place of an unusable or severely sloped yard.

Balance your requirements

With any deck, a critical issue is the balance of privacy, sun, and shade. It can be tricky to get this relationship just right. While privacy is important, you don't want to block any good views, air flow, or sunshine. It takes careful planning to figure out which areas you want to shade from the sun and protect from the wind.

Once you've detailed your goals and have a rough plan of what you need, list all the accessories needed to provide comfortable outdoor living for your family. Whether it's a selection of tables, chairs, and hammocks, or equipment such as grills and cooking extras, or even a child's playhouse, you need to note it all. You'll use this information later when you figure out how big to make your deck.

Planning ahead for storage will keep clutter from becoming a problem once the deck is finished. Make a detailed list of all the stor-

Protection from the sun can be provided by careful positioning so that the house casts shade on the deck during the afternoon, or by building a permanent structure such as a pergola or an arbor planted with a bushy vine.

age you'll need. Benches with lift-up seats are great for stashing toys, chair cushions, candles, and other accessories, and there's no better way to store cooking utensils than in a built-in cabinet or two. The space under a high deck is an obvious place to stash deck furniture and other bulky items during the winter. Low decks can be designed with a trap door in the decking and a built-in box below to hold hoses, gardening equipment, and empty planting containers. Patio pots overflowing with colorful flowers are a must-have accessory for most people, so try to build in convenient storage for gardening supplies.

This is also the time to work out your lighting plan. Low-voltage lights are a good choice because they're easy to install. While they don't put out a lot of light, they shine enough to highlight the deck and make walking up and down the stairs safer. If you'll be building a multi-level deck, good stair lighting is essential.

The right lighting can make your deck as comfortable to use at night as it is by day. Low-voltage lights are easy to install yourself.

A pool deck's primary use is obvious, but carefully consider all the functions you want the deck to serve and make sure your design accommodates them. Here, a fence replaces a deck railing, providing privacy as well as security.

Get the picture

To help you imagine what the new deck will look like in relation to the house and yard, shoot photos of the site and enlarge them. Lay tracing paper over the photos and sketch your different deck ideas.

Choosing the Site

Take a good look at your yard and compare its features to your list of priorities. Somewhere in your yard is a single best place for the deck, and it's your job to find it. A flat yard will present more siting options than a sloping yard, but decks can successfully be built in yards with fairly steep drop-offs. In fact, building a deck is sometimes the only way to reclaim what would otherwise be useless yard space.

What if your lot is covered with trees? Don't worry – decks can wrap around one or several trees, or can completely surround a tree. Just construct the hole so there's enough room for you to trim back the deck boards as the tree grows – typically, a 4-inch gap between tree and deck will do the trick.

While you're evaluating the site, think about drainage. Standing water attracts mosquitoes, and continually damp conditions encourage fungi and mildew which will rot the wood. A layer of several inches of gravel will help improve drainage under any deck. Lay a sheet of landscape fabric beneath the gravel and you'll also prevent most weeds from poking through.

Views and privacy

Ideally, you should be able to appreciate your deck from inside the house as much as from the outside. To do that, you'll have to consider how the deck will relate to existing views as well as to the landscape. If you're trying to play up a dramatic view, consider a deck that wraps around the house, and design an open-style railing. If the deck is close to the ground, plan on low plantings that will enhance the deck without detracting from the view. For high decks on heavily wooded sites, you may have to thin out some trees to enhance the view. To disguise an eyesore (or a busy street), enclose at least part of the deck with a closed railing and go for taller plantings.

You'll need to balance the privacy you want against any views you stand to lose. A

A good site map shows the location of the deck as well as the trees, shrubs, and any other nearby landscape features. It shows sun and shade patterns for as many seasons as the deck will be in use. It also describes the views from all sides of the deck – good, bad, and ugly. Traffic patterns in the yard and through the house (to access the deck) should also be included.

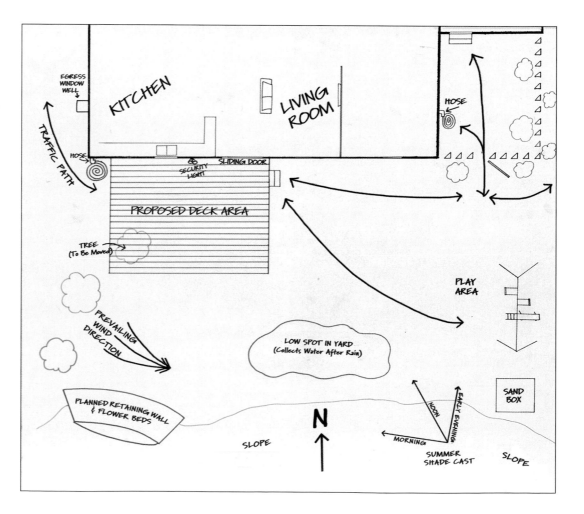

A privacy fence *gives a sense of seclusion, while the pergola overhead breaks up the light, giving sunbathers the choice between full sun, partial shade, and full shade.*

tall, solid-wood railing will give you total privacy, but it will also obstruct all views and may make you feel boxed in. A better choice is to use a railing with fairly close slats and substitute a tall privacy screen for a section of railing wherever you want more privacy. If you have a multi-level deck and want to conceal the level used for sunning or relaxing in a spa, you only need to block off that particular area. Finally, consult your site plan to make sure that the railings and privacy structures won't deprive your deck of too much sun.

Railings and privacy screens around a deck probably will also be visible from inside the house, and they could block the light, or interfere with views you enjoy. As a planning technique, you can prop up 2x4s to represent the corners of the deck

structure and fencing to represent the railing. Then go inside the house and see how much of the view is blocked. By incorporating steps and different deck levels, you'll probably be able to preserve most of the view. An afternoon spent experimenting and sketching will be a good investment in the success of your deck project.

Deck meets house

As your design develops, make sure to check that the style of the deck works with the style of the house. A curvy deck might look out of place on a boxy Cape-style house, but it could work perfectly with a contemporary house. Likewise, glass-paneled railings could enhance the look of a modern home but might detract from one with a traditional style.

Staining the deck railing to match the house siding is a surefire way to unify the deck and the house. So is building a multi-level deck that flows around a portion of the house and invites entry from several rooms. Don't forget that your new deck will probably require some landscaping. New grass, shrubs, or flower beds will ease the transition from the deck to the rest of the yard.

The light below

If you have ground-floor rooms and you plan a second-story deck, be sure that the deck doesn't block all the daylight. A four-foot overhang won't block your view of the sky from the rooms below, but a 12-foot overhang probably will leave you in the gloom. A multi-level deck is one way to solve this problem, as is a narrow deck leading to a larger expanse away from the downstairs windows. You can also frame window-sized openings in the deck (they'll need railings), about a foot away from the house; they'll act as skylights for the rooms down below.

Trees and decks *can make good neighbors. Just make sure the tree is healthy to begin with and stays that way. Don't cut into the roots during construction, and leave some breathing room around the trunk. Here, the insert can be replaced as the tree grows.*

This multi-level deck allows light and air to enter the ground floor of the house. Multiple staircases provide access to either level of the deck from the yard, as well as easy movement between levels.

Traffic patterns

Adding a deck is bound to rearrange the traffic patterns in both your home and your yard. It may seem obvious, but you should locate the main access to the deck through a public room. Bedroom access is fine when it leads to a private reading or sunbathing area, but you wouldn't want people traipsing through on their way to the barbecue. Typically, the closer you can locate the main access to the kitchen, the more convenient outdoor cooking and cleanup will be. If your kitchen already has a window on the back side of the house, you may be able to turn it into a doorway. Wherever you locate deck access, sliding glass doors or French doors bring more of the outside in than single doors do, and they will also help to integrate the deck with the rest of the house.

Depending on where you locate the stairs, the deck will change exterior traffic patterns, too. Low decks may have a series of wide, cascading stairs that offer access to the yard from several points. These types of stairs also provide extra seating and are a great place to park

planters. Higher decks will need at least one staircase to allow people to get down to the yard. A long run of stairs can be broken up with a landing, which also allows the stairs to turn.

It's important to plot out the route between the stairs and the driveway, garage, existing outbuildings, and children's play spaces. While you want good access to these areas, you don't want the stairs to become an obstacle or to block a major traffic path. Unless you absolutely have to, don't make people walk around the entire deck to get to the stairs. Try to locate the stairs so they're convenient and somewhat central, while at the same time routing people away from private areas of the deck. Likewise, you probably will not want to lead people past undesirable views, such as trash cans or a clothesline. To avoid traffic jams on the deck, keep benches, planters, lounge furniture, barbecue grills, sandboxes, and similar items clear of the traffic path.

The design and finish of the rail complement the house trim and help blend the deck with the house. A larger, more imposing deck would have changed the character of the house.

Hidden access

It's easy to forget about hose bibs, meters, and downspouts when planning a deck. Fortunately, none of these things is too difficult or expensive to relocate if you do have to deck over it.

A good alternative is a removable piece of decking, held in place by the joists and perhaps some extra blocking.

Climate Considerations

While cooling breezes are welcome on a hot summer day, gale-force winds are another matter. Study the direction of the prevailing winds before siting your deck. You may need to plant trees or tall shrubs as windbreaks, or even design and build a windscreen into the deck.

Sun and shade patterns throughout the various seasons should already be on your site plan. It's easy to shield a deck from boiling afternoon sun, but the only way to make sure you will have as much (or as little) sun as you want is to plan for it during the design phase.

A deck with a roof not only provides shade, it also allows you to remain outdoors during rain showers. If your climate features annoying insects, you'll also be able to screen the covered portion of the deck. The key to outdoor climate control is choices, so you can find the right amount of shelter for the conditions of the moment. Consider what makes you comfortable outdoors then design features into the deck that will provide that comfort. Otherwise, you may find yourself using the deck far less than you had planned.

The space beneath low decks may suffer from a lack of air circulation, so don't cover the space between the platform structure and the ground with solid wood. Either leave the space open, or use lattice to let drying breezes through. Unless water pools under the deck (and it shouldn't if you grade and shovel several inches of gravel under the deck for drainage), the spaces between the deck boards will allow adequate ventilation.

Between the screened porch and the sunny deck, this house has lots of choices for finding outdoor comfort. The screened porch has bubble skylights to let in more light.

House optional

Though decks customarily attach to the house, they don't have to. You can build a freestanding deck to create a sitting place anywhere you like. It can be an island in the garden or woods, or a destination at the end of a path. If you have a pond or an interesting view from one area of your lot, consider building a low deck there.

You could make a deck out of stone or brick (but then it would probably be called a patio). Whether you choose to build with wood, stone, or brick depends on whether you're more comfortable with woodworking tools or with masonry tools. It also depends on the terrain. A wooden deck on piers can rise above whatever's on the ground, but for a patio you'll have to level the ground first.

This freestanding, ground-level deck overhangs a ravine and a creek. As well as adding usable space, it makes a destination out of a feature of the landscape.

Design Elements

Among the important decisions you will have to make during deck design is whether you want a single-level or a multi-level deck. Multi-level decks create outdoor rooms, which can be used for a variety of purposes. The top level makes a natural play space for young children, since it's close to the house. A second or third level can be for

This multi-level deck features broad steps with low benches and railings. This structure offers many different spaces for people and plants, and it's also visually interesting.

cooking and dining, or a spa. Multi-level decks look more interesting and, when properly designed, can give the backyard a unique look. They're also a good way to squeeze more deck onto a sloping lot. Cost is another benefit. If your dreams are bigger than your wallet, multi-level decks can be constructed a section at a time, spreading the cost over a number of years.

If a single-level deck is more appropriate for your house, it doesn't have to be boring. Many decks feature an angular design because it's an easy way to add architectural interest to an otherwise plain deck. Unusual railings and built-ins also offer visual appeal.

Decking options

The decking you put down will become the visual focus of the deck. It can be simple – a series of boards nailed perpendicular to the joists – or a more complex pattern. Because different decking patterns call for different understructures, it is important to decide on the decking pattern during the design phase.

There are several interesting decking patterns to choose from. More complicated decking patterns will require a different joist layout than a simple decking pattern. For a basket weave effect, modular mini-decks are placed at right angles to one another. This is a good way to make use of short decking boards, but it involves more cutting. Picture-frame decks are attractive, too. A herringbone pattern, another popular choice, takes advantage of a diagonal layout. Like other intricate patterns, herringbone decking patterns require more lumber to allow for waste in cutting the boards to the pattern; they also require more lumber for the understructure.

Railings

Deck rails must be strong and spaced closely enough to keep people – especially children – from falling off. Most building codes specify that railings be at least 36 inches tall with openings no more than 4 inches wide. Code doesn't usually require a railing for decks less than 30 inches above grade. However, consider adding one just for safety's sake. As an alternative, a low, built-in bench would also serve to warn people away from the edge of the deck.

Benches, planters, angled steps and a pergola add visual appeal and useful "rooms" to this otherwise plain deck.

Looks are important, too. Most railing patterns are variations of three basic styles: post and rail, picket, and panel. The variation comes in the size and type of materials, and the sizes and spacing of the parts. To maximize views, railing panels can be made from clear acrylic set in wooden frames.

Choose a railing style carefully, keeping in mind that the more complex the design, the more time-consuming (and more expensive) it will be to construct. Some designs will also make it more difficult to sweep leaves and shovel snow off the deck.

***Elaborate deck designs**, like this airy gazebo, can be blended with their surroundings by a carefully chosen railing pattern.*

Stairs, spas, and built-ins

Stairs may be straight, winding, or have one or more landings. Winding stairs and stairs with landings are most versatile, because they can change direction as needed. They're especially useful to avoid a long run of stairs in sloped yards. Although stairs with closed risers look neater and more formal, deck stairs typically have open risers to make it easier to clear off leaves and snow.

Plan your stairs as carefully as you plan the deck. They should match the style of the deck, not look like they were just stuck on as a way to get from here to there. Try to keep stairways in proportion to the deck. A narrow stairway leading off a broad deck will look out of scale. Remember that you can make deck stairs as wide as you want, creating space for built-in cabinets, benches, or

Railing options

You've got dozens of choices for railings, and they're not all wood. With a little ingenuity and work, you can create a rail-ing that accents your deck and integrates it with the style of your house.

***A pipe railing** fills in between wooden posts, creating an airy, open look that hardly interferes with the view. These pipes are brushed chrome.*

***This curved railing** echoes the soft shapes of the trees and landscape, making an inviting deck that blends into the forest. The curves were made by bending thin strips of wood and gluing them together.*

***Painted lattice** offers a lot of privacy while still admitting plenty of light and air. Wooden lattice is easiest to paint with an airless sprayer. While you could assemble your own lattice, it's a stock product at most home centers.*

A spa can be the centerpiece of a lavish deck. This one has a wet bar, built-in planters accented with the same tile as the bartop, and night lighting.

planters. Low decks can utilize a series of broad, low steps which offer access to the deck from many points and also make convenient locations for patio pots.

Freestanding spas and hot tubs are popular additions to decks, but the deck framing has to be beefed up to support their weight when filled with water – on average, about 4,000 pounds. You may want built-in seating near the spa, a privacy screen, and perhaps a sunscreen overhead. Spas also need plumbing, wiring, and storage for chemicals and tools.

Benches are the simplest built-ins for decks. In many situations a bench can replace a section of railing, and can be built with the same materials. Other useful built-ins include picnic tables, storage boxes, counters, planters, and lighting posts.

A built-in bench fills in for a section of railing on this shady deck. Seat rails and diagonal braces support the seat, while a scrap of lattice accents the arm support.

STRUCTURAL REQUIREMENTS

Like the floor in your house, *a deck is a platform of joists covered with boards. It's usually fastened to the house along one side, with most of its weight resting on posts supported by concrete footings that are buried in the earth. Although a deck is simpler than enclosed construction, it has many of the same elements as a house, and it must also meet most of the same building regulations. This means you'll need to work closely with your local building department to make sure your plans satisfy the building code and that your construction work passes inspection.*

Parts of a Deck

Although a deck may contain hundreds of pieces of wood, hardware, and fasteners, everything goes together logically. A deck consists of footings that support beams and/or joists, which support the decking. A rim joist connects the free ends of the field joists, and also provides a secure anchor for railings, stairs, privacy screens, and overhead structures. Nails, screws, bolts, and metal connectors hold the whole thing together.

Ledger board

For all but freestanding decks, the rim joist alongside the house is called a ledger board. It's a long piece of lumber fastened to the side of the house, and it's the first piece of the deck to be installed. It has two functions: It supports the joists and it ties the deck to the house. Expect to remove some siding to make space for the ledger board, and be sure to install metal flashing so water can't get into the wall.

Concrete footings

Once the ledger board is in, the footings follow. Decks in cold climates are usually supported by poured concrete footings. Local building codes specify the diameter of the footings and the distance they must extend below the frost line to prevent them from heaving. In warmer climates, where frost heave is not a problem, you can use precast pier blocks set into concrete pads.

Posts

Pressure-treated deck posts can be cast directly in concrete footings, but they'll last longer if they're fastened to the concrete above ground. This allows water to drain so the wood doesn't rot. Your local building code may specify a particular connection, so be sure to check. To ensure that all the posts turn out to be the same height, they're often installed long and trimmed to length later.

Beams

Beams rest on top of the posts. They're usually made by nailing two or three 2x10 or 2x12 planks together. If the beams will be visible, solid wood might look better, but solid wood is expensive, heavy to maneuver, and often difficult to find.

Joists

The joists spread the load of people (live load) and the weight of the deck itself plus deck furniture and accessories (dead load) across the beams. On a simple deck, the joists usually run perpendicular to the side of the house and to the deck boards. The outside joists are called the perimeter or rim joists. Doubling up the rim joists adds stability to the deck. Depending on the span of the deck, you'll need 2x6s, 2x8s, 2x10s, or 2x12s for joists.

Decking

The decking is the floor of the deck. Taste, budget, and structural requirements all will affect your selection of deck boards. Your choices include lumber species, board thickness (1⅛ or 1½ inches), and board width (usually, narrower boards will develop fewer cracks).

Fasteners

Metal fasteners and connectors join all the various pieces of wood together. You'll be using more nails,

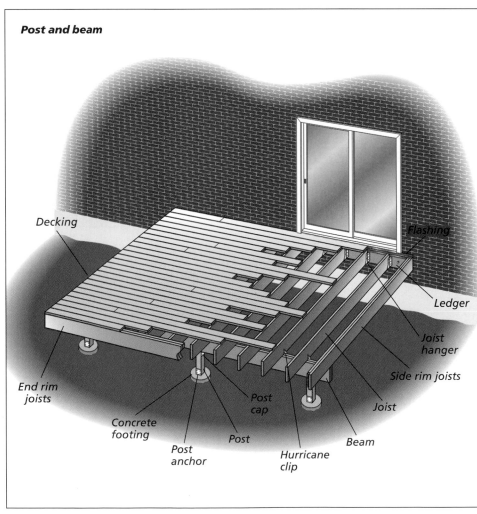

Post and beam

Decking

Flashing

Ledger

Joist hanger

Side rim joists

Joist

End rim joists

Concrete footing

Post cap

Post

Beam

Post anchor

Hurricane clip

In post and beam construction, the joists rest on a beam that's supported by posts. This allows the joists to cantilever beyond the beams. The rim joist ties the free ends of the field joists together, but it doesn't carry their load.

bolts, screws, and fasteners than you thought possible when building even a small deck. While you could build a deck entirely with nails, bolts and screws, specialized connectors such as joist hangers and post anchors hold better than nails alone and are also much easier to install.

Beams or Not?

There are two basic ways to carry the weight of the deck to its support posts: post and beam, or post and rim joist. Each method has its strong points, so the one you choose depends on the details of your particular situation.

In post and rim joist construction, the rim joist does double duty. It rests directly on top of the posts, acting as a beam, but it also ties the ends of the field joists together, same as any other rim joist. This puts the posts right out at the corners of the deck, with intermediate posts spaced along the front edge. This construction is economical because it uses less lumber than a post and beam deck. However, it may not be as strong, because the joist hangers must carry the full load of the deck plus everyone and everything on it.

In post and beam construction, the joists rest on a beam, which sits on top of the posts. One advantage is that the joists can cantilever beyond the beam by up to two feet. As a result, the posts sit back from the edge of the deck, more or less out of sight. A disadvantage is that you'll also need a rim joist, so this construction uses more wood and is more expensive than a post and rim joist deck.

In complex, multi-level decks, you'll find yourself combining both kinds of construc-

tion. A wide deck with a long joist span may have both kinds of support beneath a single platform – post and rim joist at the outer edge, with an intermediate beam resting on posts under the middle of the joists.

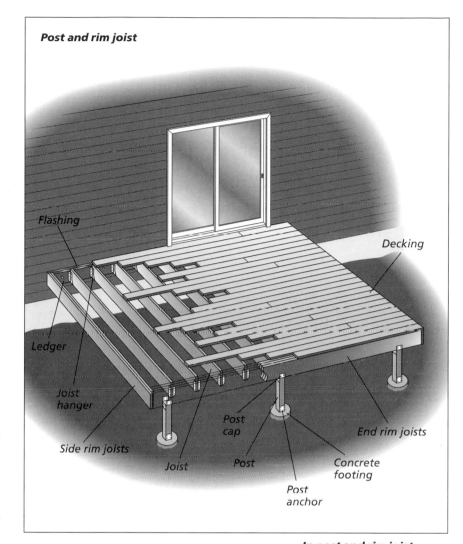

Post and rim joist

Labels: Flashing, Ledger, Joist hanger, Side rim joists, Joist, Post, Post cap, Post anchor, Concrete footing, End rim joists, Decking

In post and rim joist construction, the joists attach directly to the face of the rim joist, which rests on top of the posts. The rim joist not only ties the free ends of the joists together, it also doubles as a beam, carrying the load down to the posts.

Notches and nails

Many wooden joints require sawing notches in one piece of wood so it fits around another piece. When making load-bearing notches, or housings, never cut away more than half of the thickness of the wood. Think about which piece is carrying the load, and what stresses the wood and fasteners are likely to bear. Whenever possible, transmit the load downward by resting one piece of wood on top of another. Use nails, bolts, and screws to fasten pieces of wood together, not to hold them up.

Footings

The footings anchor the deck to the ground, distribute its weight, and protect wooden posts from direct contact with the soil. The required depth and diameter of the footings varies from one part of the country to another, depending on soil type and how deep (or whether) the ground is likely to freeze. In general, the footing should extend 6 inches below the frost line. The size and weight of the deck will also affect the diameter of the footings. Make sure you're in compliance with your local code, because your deck will have to pass inspection.

Although the footings have to extend below the frost line, you can decide whether to pour the concrete up to ground level, or whether to set pressure-treated wooden posts on frost-line footings and backfill around them with gravel. Concrete is heavy and it may be difficult to transport it to the deck site, but in most situations it's the best choice. Although it's easier to just backfill the wooden posts with dirt or gravel, wood is al-

ways liable to rot when it's in contact with soil, and even pressure-treated wood rated for ground contact doesn't last forever.

Concrete footings should always be wider at the bottom than at the top. If the footing flares out at the top, it's liable to be pushed out of the ground by winter soil movement. If you can't dig a straight hole – or better yet, one that bells out at the bottom – you'll have to use fiberboard form tubes. A tube also allows you to bring the top of the concrete 2 to 6 inches above ground level, keeping the post base above wet soil. The most common size of form tube is 12 inches in diameter, but the local building code will tell you what's necessary in your area.

Plan to use galvanized metal anchors to connect the posts to the footings. Most types have to be embedded in the wet concrete, though some can be fastened with bolts set in holes drilled after the concrete cures. Post anchors not only make a secure connection, they'll also raise the wood off the concrete, which helps it stay dry.

After digging the hole to depth, use a clam-shell digger to widen the bottom of the hole into a bell shape. This helps stabilize the footings. Try not to disturb the soil at the bottom of the hole.

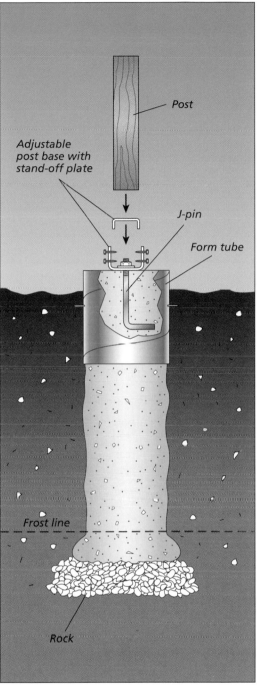

Concrete footings *should extend below the frost line and bell out at the bottom to resist frost heave. At the top, the concrete extends above grade to keep the wood post away from wet soil. (A precast pier block set into wet concrete at ground level does the same job.)*

When a form tube is used, it must stop short of the base so the concrete can spread into the bell. The tube is cut, plumbed, and spiked into the surrounding soil before the concrete is poured.

In this footing system, each post rests in a metal bracket that is attached to the footing with a J-bolt.

Posts

The job of the deck posts is to carry the load from the rest of the deck down to the footings. While decks are designed with fun in mind, safety must always come first. Remember that building codes specify minimum sizes for posts and beams. When in doubt, overbuild.

Materials

Pressure-treated wood is usually used for deck posts because it resists decay. Most codes specify .40 pressure-treated lumber for deck posts, but many builders recommend beefing up the decay resistance by using .60. The rating refers to how much preservative (in pounds per cubic foot) has been forced into the wood.

Sizing and spacing

The longer the spans between structural components, the bigger the components have to be. This is why you have to look at the rest of the deck before sizing and spacing the posts. For example, 4x4 posts that can support a low deck may bend when installed under a deck more than 8 feet high. In general, use 6x6 posts for any deck over 4 feet off the ground. Any time you will be including a spa or hot tub, get professional advice, because you'll be propping up a couple of tons of water.

How far apart you space posts depends on the size of the beams. Keep posts a maximum distance of 6 feet apart under 4x6 and 3x8 beams. Posts supporting 4x8 and 3x10 beams should be no more than 8 feet apart; those supporting 4x10 or 3x12 beams can go 10 feet apart.

Bracing

Diagonal 2x4 bracing keeps the posts plumb during construction. As soon as you install a few joists, you can remove the bracing if it's in your way. Otherwise, leave it in place until the job is done.

Decks carrying heavy loads, decks that project more than 16 feet from the house, and decks higher than 12 feet will all require permanent bracing. The braces convert the unstable T-shaped connection between post and beam to a stable triangle. Use 2x4 braces across distances of 8 feet and under; use 2x6s for wider spans. Bolt or lag-screw the braces in place. Cross-bracing can also be made out of steel cable, steel rod, or angle iron.

Sizing Beams and Joists

Beams and joists transfer the load of the deck to the ground via the posts. Pouring footings for posts is a lot of work, so the more distance your joists and beams can span unsupported, the fewer posts you'll need. However, longer spans call for bigger pieces of

Beam sizes: Once you decide how far apart to space your posts, calculate beam size from this chart. These values are for Douglas fir and southern yellow pine; deduct 20% for redwood and cedar.

Beam size, spacing, and spans

Space between beams	Beam size	Beam span between posts
4'	4x6	6'0"
	4x8	10'0"
	4x10	12'0"
	4x12	14'0"
6'	4x6	5'6"
	4x8	9'0"
	4x10	11'2"
	4x12	13'0"
8'	4x6	–
	4x8	8'0"
	4x10	10'0"
	4x12	12'0"
10'	4x6	–
	4x8	6'0"
	4x10	8'0"
	4x12	10'0"

wood, which cost more. So what you have to do is design the most economical combination of beams and joists without compromising the strength of the deck.

These tables will help you to calculate dimensions according to span and load. However, it's a mistake to engineer things too close to the line. Your strategy should be to overbuild whenever you aren't sure what size material to use, and to check your plans with your building inspector.

While we could go into a lot of detail about wood species, the important thing to know is that Douglas fir and southern pine are the strongest construction materials, while redwood is the lightest and weakest. Allowable spans in redwood are about 20% less than for Douglas fir and southern pine. Pressure treating does not affect the strength

of the wood one way or the other. Large knots can seriously weaken structural lumber, so even though the grading system should take care of that, keep an eye out and reject any wood that doesn't look right to you.

This point may seem obvious, but joists and beams always go on edge, with their widest dimension in the up and-and-down direction. The vertical depth of the plank is what gives it resistance to bending under load.

Although it's typical to build a deck from the ground up, you calculate post spacing, beam dimensions, and joist sizes from the top down. Remember that decking and beams run perpendicular to joists, so achieving a particular look with the decking will determine the structure required beneath. The information on these pages is based on live loads of 60 pounds per square foot of decking. That allows for the weight of people at a very crowded barbecue party or about two feet of wet snow, but it doesn't allow for spas.

Joist spacing and spans

Joist spacing depends on the species and thickness of the deck boards. Decking made from 5/4 and 2x lumber generally calls for joists spaced on 16-inch centers.

The taller the joist, the more distance it can span without support. Doubling up the thickness of joists does not increase the distance they can span, but increasing their depth does. In general, 2x6 joists can span 7 feet, 2x8 joists can span 10 feet, and 2x10 joists can span 12 feet. It's normally safe to cantilever joists two feet without additional bracing.

Joist size, spacing, and spans

Joist size	Joist spacing and span	
	16" O.C.	24" O.C.
2x6	9'9"	7'11"
2x8	12'10"	10'6"
2x10	16'5"	13'4"

Joist sizes: Once you decide how far apart to space your beams, calculate joist size from this chart. These values are for Douglas fir and southern yellow pine; deduct 20% for redwood and cedar.

Beam spans

Like joists, beam spans depend more on the depth of the material than on its thickness. Once you know joist span, you'll be able to figure out how many beams you'll need, and their distance from each other. The next step is to locate the posts by dividing the length of the beams more or less equally, then use the tables to figure out the beam depth. By working back and forth, you'll be able to arrive at the most economical combination for your deck design.

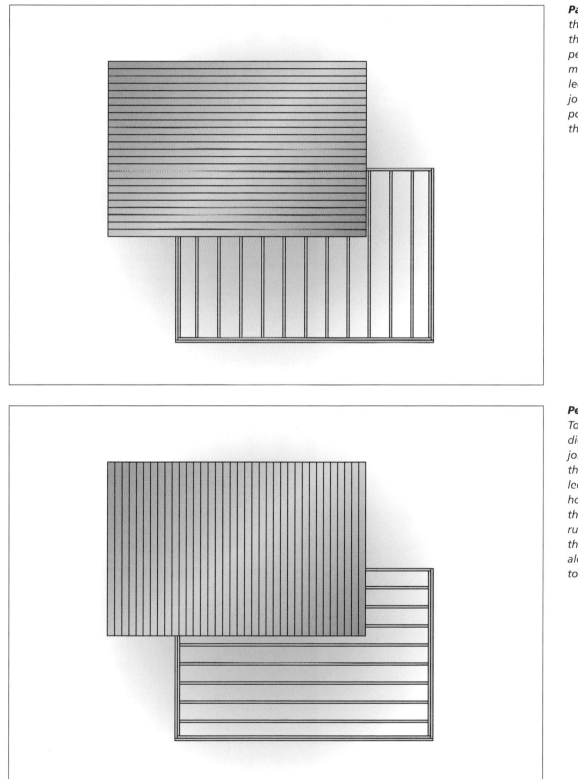

Parallel decking. *When the decking runs parallel to the house, the joists run perpendicular. This is the most typical joist layout. The ledger board supports the joists along the house, while posts and a beam support the far edge.*

Perpendicular decking. *To run the decking perpendicular to the house, the joists must be parallel to the house. In this case, the ledger ties the deck to the house but does not support the joists. Posts and beams running perpendicular to the house must be installed along both sides of the deck to support the joist ends.*

A doubled joist supports a single-board picture frame. The ends of the decking boards are nailed to one joist, while the other supports the edge of the picture-frame board.

Blocking

Blocking is cross-pieces nailed between the joists for stability. Without it, the joists may twist sideways under load, and the deck is liable to have more bounce than you'll find comfortable. Blocking also acts as nailers to help support the decking, and is often necessary for decorative decking patterns.

Make blocking from the same material you use for joists. Cut it to fit the actual spaces between joists, because bowed lumber will change the nominal space of 14½ inches between joists on 16-inch centers, and 22½ inches for joists on 24-inch centers. Usually you'll be able to get quite a few pieces of blocking from joist scrap.

If you want to remove bounce, install blocking every four to six feet, more or less. When you want to lay decking in some particular pattern, install blocking wherever you need it to support the decking and act as nailers. In some situations (picture-frame decking, for example) you may need to install blocking to support decking that runs parallel to the joists and to support mitered boards that meet in corners.

Sometimes you'll see diagonal cross-braces between the joists, where you would expect to see blocking. They'll have the same structural effect, but they're a lot more difficult to install, and they don't create any useful nailing surface.

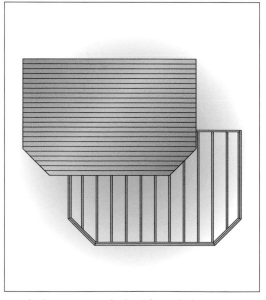

Angled corners. A deck with angled corners needs rim joists cut to match. Joists that meet the angled rim joist must either be mitered or joined with special joist hangers (see page 31).

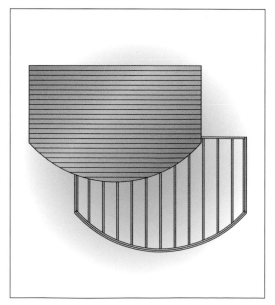

Curved deck. From a structural point of view, a curved deck is the same as a straight deck, except for the shape of the rim joist.

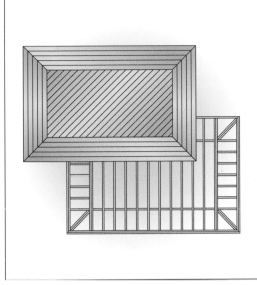

Picture frame. Set joists and blocking along the perimeter, with diagonal nailers in the corners to support the mitered ends of the picture-frame boards.

Basket weave. Decking laid in a basket weave pattern requires a joist structure to match. Blocking and doubled joists support decking that runs parallel to the joists and board ends where the pattern changes direction.

Decking

Your deck gets a lot of its character from the decking pattern you choose. However, you can't come along at the end and do whatever you want, because the decking has to be supported and fastened to joists or nailers. This is why you've got to plan the decking pattern from the outset.

Deck boards can be made from 2x4, 2x6, or 5/4x6 lumber. Although 2x4 decking requires a lot more nailing than 2x6, you can mix the two widths for a decorative effect. Most 5/4 decking comes with a rounded edge, and some types come with a preservative already applied. Boards wider than 6 inches shouldn't be used for decking, because normal wood movement pulling against the fasteners will cause them to split. Diagonal decking may call for thicker wood than regular decking, because the diagonal distance between joists placed 16 inches on center is 22 inches.

Whenever possible, buy deck boards that will span the full distance without needing to be spliced. If you must join the decking, make sure you stagger the joints so they don't all land on the same joist. Where the decking design calls for all the decking joints to fall on the same joist (herringbone, for example) plan on installing a doubled joist to support the decking ends.

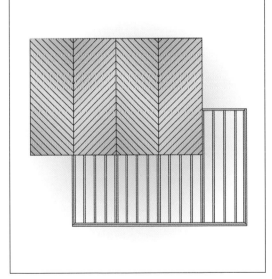

Herringbone. Double the joists to create nailers under the mitered ends of the decking.

Stairs and Railings

While outdoor steps are often deeper and lower than indoor stairs, it's still important that each step in a flight be the same height and depth as all the others.

The vertical height from one step to the next is the rise, which should be somewhere between 4 inches and 7 inches. The total height of the flight divided by the number of risers equals the height of each riser.

The horizontal distance, or the depth of the tread, is called the run; it should measure between 10 inches and 18 inches. Make up the depth by combining 2x4s with 2x6s. Riser height plus tread depth should total 17 to 21 inches, which is a comfortable distance for most people. This means that steps with a deep tread have a low rise, while high-rising steps have shallow treads. The width of the tread shouldn't be less than 30 inches.

Stringers

The stringers support the steps. The outside stringers can be cut out to accept the treads, or they can be solid planks with metal or wooden cleats nailed on. Stairs wider than 3 feet need a central stringer in addition to the two outside ones. For total runs up to 6 feet, you can use 2x10s for stringers, unless you want a deep tread. In that case, and for runs greater than 6 feet, use 2x12s.

Deck railings

You're always better off to add railings around your deck, even when it is low and code might let you get away without them. Railings have to be sturdy, because people will lean on them and sit on them. The space between the railing and the deck can be filled in with vertical spindles or with horizontal railings, depending on the look you want. For child safety, the building code specifies 4 inches as the maximum opening between spindles.

Railings typically consist of 4x4 posts spaced about 4 feet apart and bolted or lag-screwed to the rim joists. Handrails should be made of 2x4s or 2x6s, and spindles of 2x4s or 2x2s. Railings should rise between 34 and 38 inches above the edge of the deck.

This typical stair has three 2x12 notched stringers joined by 2x6 backers at the top and bottom. The top stringer backer is screwed to a stringer header fastened beneath the rim joist. Two 2x6s make up the 11-inch treads.

The 4x4 railing posts are bolted to the rim joists; on the stairs, they are bolted to the stringers, not to the treads. The cap rail is a 2x6; on the stair rail it is supplemented by a graspable handrail, as required by local code.

Post   Bottom rail   Cap rail   Graspable handrail   Spindle

Stringer header   Stringer backer   Stringer   Stringer backer   Tread

Stair railings

The building code requires a handrail on any flight of steps that rises more than 30 inches. Stair railings must follow the same slope as the stringers. They're usually constructed in the same way as deck railings, with the posts securely fastened to the stringers or to the rim joist. The building code requires an easy-to-grasp railing between 1¼ and 2 inches in diameter on at least one side.

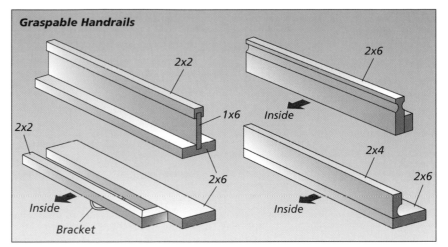

Graspable Handrails

A graspable handrail should be 1¼ to 2 inches in diameter. You can attach a stock handrail (available at home centers and lumberyards) or create a custom design to match the style of your deck. The designs shown here can be made from common lumber sizes; some require using a router to create a groove for fingertips.

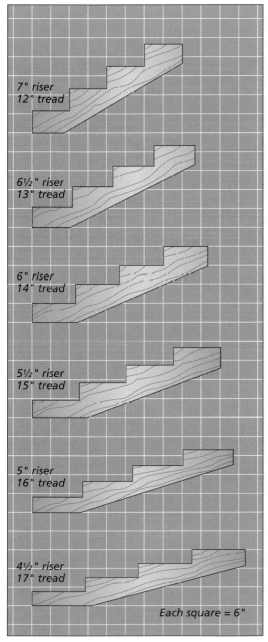

7" riser
12" tread

6½" riser
13" tread

6" riser
14" tread

5½" riser
15" tread

5" riser
16" tread

4½" riser
17" tread

Each square = 6"

Combined rise and run *for each step should total between 17 and 21 inches. Altering the rise and run ratio changes the amount of height or distance a staircase will span.*

Bolt railing posts *to rim joists and stringers. Notching the post so it sits on the deck or tread surface helps make a strong joint.*

Railing posts can also be notched *and attached inside the rim joist. Decking notched to fit around the post gives a neat appearance.*

Railings and code

Building code specifies a 4-inch maximum opening between spindles. The 4-inch spacing is required so toddlers can't squeeze their bodies through openings. Don't sacrifice child safety for the sake of appearance.

Along the stairs, the bottom rail can be no more than 6 inches above any point of the tread. A simple way to test this is with a 6-inch ball or cardboard circle.

Privacy Screens

A privacy screen is just a tall railing, and it should be designed and built the same way. The support posts shouldn't be farther than 4 feet apart and must be bolted securely to the understructure of the deck. If there are deck posts near the privacy screen, another option is to run the deck posts long and use them to support the privacy screen. You will probably still have to attach some intermediate posts to the rim joist.

The fill should be an open lattice to admit light and air while providing some visual screening. In windy locations, you might want a solid Plexiglas screen to make the deck more comfortable without blocking the view, but be sure to brace it securely so it doesn't blow down.

An overhead structure, often called a pergola, creates partial shade and a sense of enclosure. Here the same 6x6 posts that support the privacy screen hold up the rafters overhead.

Overhead Structures

An open roof overhead is a lightweight version of the deck itself. It doesn't have to support the same loads so you can use smaller dimensioned lumber, but the attachment to the deck or house still has to be secure and sturdy. When the roof attaches to the side of the house, lag-screw a ledger to the house studs and be sure to add metal flashing. The posts that support the deck itself can run long to support the overhead structure, or new posts can be notched and bolted to the rim joists. Local code in high-wind regions will probably require the use of hurricane ties to keep the beams and rafters from lifting off in high winds; in earthquake zones these are known as seismic connectors.

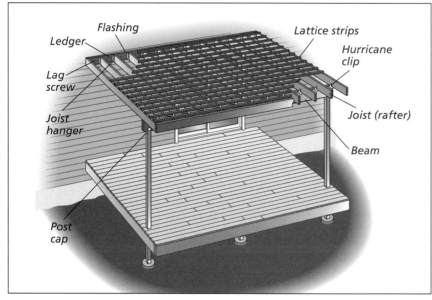

Attach overhead structures to the house with a ledger board. The beams and rafters correspond to the deck beams and joists, but they don't have to be as large because they don't support as much weight.

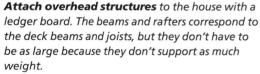

An overhead structure may also be freestanding, supported by posts that rise from the ground or from the deck understructure, and joined with the same kind of metal connectors.

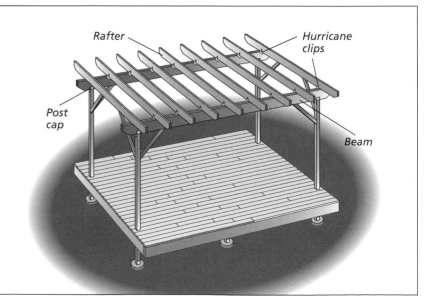

MATERIALS

It's safe to say that 99% of all decks are made of wood. *For the back-yard builder, wood has a number of advantages, starting with its workability: you can cut it and nail it together using familiar tools. However, wood is susceptible to weather damage and to decay, so you still need to decide between a naturally resistant species, such as redwood, and wood that has been chemically treated to increase its durability. You'll also need to choose the appropriate fasteners and finish for outdoor duty.*

Working with pressure-treated lumber

The chemicals forced into pressure-treated wood are hazardous. To avoid inhaling them, it's a good idea to put on a particle mask every time you pick up the saw. The chemicals may also rub off on your skin, so consider wearing work gloves.

While it may be tempting to toss pressure-treated offcuts in your wood stove or fireplace, don't. Burning not only releases chemicals into the air, it leaves deposits of heavy metals in the ashes. Either bury pressure-treated wood (avoid areas near vegetable or flower gardens) or dispose of it with the regular household trash.

Whenever you work with a power saw – whether you're cutting ordinary lumber or pressure-treated wood – wear a particle mask, safety goggles, hearing protection, and steel-toed work boots.

Lumber

When you go to the home center or lumberyard to buy wood, you'll have to decide which grade to choose. Lumber grades are regulated by trade associations of lumber producers, and vary from species to species. In general, choose structural No. 1 or No. 2 for the posts, joists, and other structural parts of your deck. For the decking, handrails, and any built-in benches, choose No. 1, select, or finish-grade material. The longevity and structural integrity of your deck depends on the wood you choose, so the lumber budget is not the place to cut corners.

After strength, the most important quality in deck-building material is the ability to withstand moisture, rot, and insects. Some woods have this ability naturally, others get it through treatment with chemical preservatives, and some are even modified with plastic.

Whether you choose a rot-resistant wood species or pressure-treated wood, you'll also have to decide about finishing it. A deck finish gives some protection from the elements. However, you will have to renew the finish every year or two.

Don't count on the finish alone to protect the wood – building the deck so water can drain is its first protection. A water-repellent finish is the second line of defense. If you don't stain the wood, weathering will turn it a soft gray or brown color, which can be rejuvenated by washing with detergent and mildewcide. But without a water repellent finish, weathering will also dry the wood and turn it splintery, opening cracks where water can enter and make it deteriorate more quickly.

The grade stamp tells you the grade of the lumber – in this example, a construction stud. The stamp also tells something about the wood dryness (S-DRY means the wood contained less than 19% moisture when it was surfaced), the wood species (WW means white wood, an assortment of species that may include hemlock, spruce, fir and white pine), the trade association that produced it (WWP means Western Wood Products Association), and the mill number (140).

Cedar and redwood

These attractive woods are naturally resistant to insects, moisture, and decay. Both are more expensive than pressure-treated lumber, and redwood is usually the more expensive of the two. Both woods come in various grades, depending on the number and types of knots. Redwood is also graded by how much heartwood or sapwood it contains – an important distinction because heartwood is

Pressure-treated lumber, usually southern pine, is green or brownish to start but fades to a dull gray after several years of exposure to the weather.

Redwood has a pinkish color when new. If left unfinished, it fades to a brownish-gray color.

Cedar ranges from white through yellow to tan in color. It turns a silvery gray as it weathers.

stronger than sapwood. Because of their expense, top-of-the-line cedar and redwood are typically used for decking, railings, and other highly visible parts of the deck, while pressure-treated lumber is used for the understructure. If you want to use these woods in the deck's understructure, use heartwood cedar or construction-grade redwood. Cedar and redwood both take finishes well.

Pressure-treated wood

There's no question that pressure-treated lumber is the most popular deck-building material around. It's readily available, inexpensive, and highly resistant to insects and rot. The preservative (usually chromated copper arsenate) gives the lumber a green or khaki color, but this can be easily covered up with stain or sealer. Some pressure-treated lumber comes prestained to match cedar or redwood. This is called brown-treated, as opposed to green-treated lumber.

The most commonly available pressure-treated wood is southern yellow pine. It absorbs the preserving chemicals easily and the treatment will penetrate just about all the way through 2x lumber. On larger timbers, such as 4x4s or 6x6s, the chemicals don't penetrate all the way to the center. You'll have to treat the cut ends by brushing on a solution of 2% copper preservative. Western pines are denser than southern yellow pine and don't absorb preservative as well, so always be sure to treat all cut surfaces.

When buying pressure-treated wood, you will have to choose among various grades.

No. 2 lumber is knottier and has grain that's more uneven than Select or No. 1, but it's perfectly fine to use in a deck understructure, where looks aren't an issue. For visible areas of the deck, upgrade to Select or No. 1 wood. Don't use any wood graded below No. 2.

Another popular pressure-treated lumber is called radius-edge decking. This wood is usually 1⅛ or 5/4 inches thick, has rounded edges, and often comes with a factory-applied water-repellent.

Lumber sizes

Construction lumber is referred to by its cross-sectional size: 2x4, 4x4, 2x6, 2x8. However, a 2x4 isn't 2 inches by 4 inches, it's closer to 1½ inches by 3½ inches. In general, there's a difference of ½ inch or ¾ inch between the wood's nominal size and its actual size after the milling and drying processes.

Length is more exact and, in construction lumber, always in 2-foot increments. An 8-foot plank measures 96 to 96½ inches long. One 16-foot plank probably will cost less than two 8-footers. However, expect to pay a premium for lumber 20 feet and longer.

Nominal size	Actual size
2x4	1½ x 3½
2x6	1½ x 5½
2x8	1½ x 7¼
2x10	1½ x 9¼
4x4	3½ x 3½
4x6	3½ x 5½

Composite wood

Part recycled plastic, part recycled waste wood, composite wood is becoming a popular decking choice because it's practically maintenance free. You can cut it and fasten it with regular woodworking tools, and it's guaranteed not to chip, crack, rot, or otherwise degrade for more than 15 years. Composite wood costs a little more than pressure-treated wood, but you save money by never having to stain or seal it. Periodic washing is required or the material may discolor; you can use any commercial deck-washing product. Although it's heavier than wood, it does not possess the same strength and should never be used for structural support.

Plastic-wood composite decking material starts out brown but soon weathers to a uniform soft gray.

Brown-treated wood takes on a lighter shade as it weathers, but it generally remains brown.

Fiberglass decking is unaffected by weather and retains its new color for many years.

Fasteners

The best nails for decks are either hot-dipped galvanized (common steel nails coated with rust-resistant zinc) or stainless steel. Stainless steel nails cost about twice as much as hot-dipped galvanized, but they are rustproof – not just rust-resistant. Your second consideration should be nail shape. Spiral- and ring-shanked nails won't pop out as readily as common nails.

Nails are designated by length, and sold by the pound. The general rule is to choose the nail that will go through the first piece of wood and at least that far again into the second piece; general construction calls for 3-inch, or 10d, nails and 3½ inch, or 16d, nails. To improve the hold, drive nails at a slight angle.

To really beef up holding power, use screws. They're also quicker to install than nails, except when you have to drill a pilot hole to avoid splitting the wood. Nail heads are less noticeable than screw heads, but nails don't provide quite as good a connection. The most common deck screw is the hot-dipped galvanized multipurpose screw, sometimes called a buglehead. For decks, the most common lengths are 2, 2½, and 3 inches.

For major structural connections, use bolts or lag screws. Because bolts accept a nut and washer, they make stronger connections than screws do. Use bolts whenever you have access to both ends of the fastener, use lag screws when you don't. Carriage bolts have a rounded head that is less obvious than a hex-head machine bolt, so use them in highly visible areas.

Use 2-inch box nails (top left) for making lightweight deck accessories. The heavier 10d nails (top right) are for general construction. The 3-inch casing nails (bottom left) are for fastening moldings and trim pieces, while the spiral nails (center) are best for attaching decking. Use joist-hanger nails (bottom right) for fastening metal connectors to structural lumber.

Stainless steel screws (left) are the strongest and most durable (the ones shown here have square-drive heads), but they cost more than galvanized deck screws (right), which also resist rust. Dacrotized screws (center) are coated with a corrosion-resistant polymer material.

Metal Connectors

Metal connectors make quick, secure joints without the need for toenailing (driving nails at an angle). Toenailing does not guarantee a strong connection, since the nail just goes through one corner of the wood; it can also create cracks where water can enter. While most connectors can be installed with 10d or 16d common nails, some connectors require special joist hanger nails, which are shorter and thicker than regular nails.

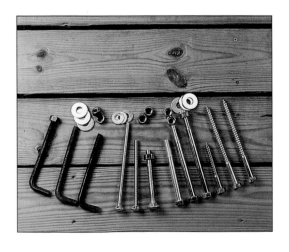

Set J-bolts (left) in concrete footings to connect wooden posts to footings. On multi-level decks, use carriage bolts or hex-head machine bolts (center) to join framing members to shared, outer posts. Use carriage bolts or heavy lag screws (right) to connect a ledger to the house framing.

Metal post bases *allow you to connect a wooden post to a concrete footing without resting the wood directly on the concrete. Some types must be embedded in wet concrete, while others bolt to embedded J-bolts. Some, like the one in the foreground, are adjustable.*

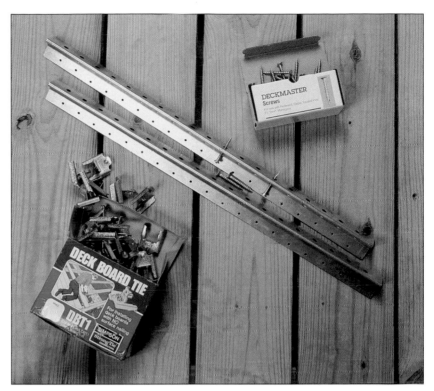

Clips and strips *are commonly used to fasten deck boards to joists from underneath. These fasteners give the deck a more finished appearance, plus there are no fastener holes to collect water.*

Post brackets *(top left) secure beams to posts. Each joint requires two brackets, one on each side of the beam. Strap ties are used to brace toenailed post to beam connections.*

In some regions, specialized metal connectors are required by the building code. In earthquake zones, the code may call for seismic connectors, which protect critical joints against uplifting and lateral flexing. In hurricane climates, the code usually specifies hurricane straps in addition to nailed or screwed connections.

Screws and nails are the usual fasteners for attaching decking to the joists, but if you don't want your fasteners to show you can use concealed hardware, such as deck strips and deck clips.

Joist connectors

Joist hangers are easier to use and stronger than nails alone, but for the strongest connection, you must drive a galvanized joist nail through every hole. Specialty joist hangers are available for most situations. They are sized to accommodate a variety of joist sizes (left, upper left and center). Some allow you to join a joist at an angle without mitering or toenailing (right). Others accommodate double joists (left, upper right).

There are also connectors for joining joists to each other and to beams. Shown below in the bottom row are (left to right) hurricane anchors used to tie field joists to beams, framing anchors used to strengthen corners where rim joists meet, and hurricane straps used to tie side rim joists to beams.

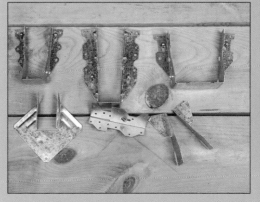

Tools

Don't go crazy assembling a deck-building tool collection, because you won't need many specialized tools. When you do buy tools, always choose the best you can afford. Cheap tools won't last very long and they'll be more difficult and less accurate to use than better-quality models.

The deck tools you'll need fall into three groups: measuring and marking tools for layout, tools for digging footings, and framing tools for cutting and assembling the deck structure. Essential layout tools include a framing square or a speed square, 25-foot tape measure, plumb bob, chalk line, and level. Foundation tools include post-hole diggers, shovels, cement mixers, and masonry tools. Framing tools include a compound miter saw, portable circular saw, reciprocating saw, framing hammer, pry bar, electric drill, and electric screwdriver. You'll also need the usual assortment of wrenches, pliers, screwdrivers, and utility knives.

Some specialty tools really speed up repetitious tasks. An air compressor with a pneumatic nailer (which you can rent), is one of the most helpful. A board bender is a specialized kind of pry bar that helps you push warped or bowed lumber into position.

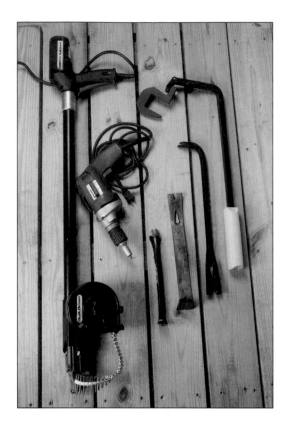

Specialty tools, such as electric screwdrivers, nail pullers, prybars, crowbars, and board benders, can really speed up a deck job. A specialized screw gun (left) allows you to drive decking screws without bending over or stopping to set each screw.

To construct a basic deck, you should have the following essential tools in your toolbox: tape measure, framing square, speed square, 4-foot level, line level, chalk line, plumb bob, hammer, chisel, circular saw, electric drill, and cordless drill.

Digging post holes is rough work but it goes easier with a two-person gas-powered auger. A one-person model will still get the job done faster than a clam-shell post-hole digger. Another alternative if you're building a large deck – hire a contractor who has power equipment for digging foundations.

PLANS and PREPARATION

Careful planning is the best way *to guarantee the success of your project. During this phase of construction you'll begin to see your deck take shape on paper, press-and-stick board, or on a computer screen. Once the final design is done, the construction work starts with estimating and ordering materials. After you're done with the paperwork, phone calls, and head-scratching (where are you going to put all this stuff anyway?), it's finally time to break ground.*

Site and Deck Plans

A site plan is the backbone of the deck plan. It helps you decide where to locate your deck and gives you an idea how it will look. Start by creating an overhead view, called a plan view, of your lot, using dimensions from the deed or from your own measurements. If you're taking your own measurements, a 50-foot reel-type tape measure works best. Next, locate your house (including door and window locations) on the plan. Measure from the house to locate and show walkways, outbuildings, trees, fences, and all other features as accurately as possible. In order to add the locations of underground utilities, such as septic systems and water, gas, electric, and telephone lines, you'll probably need to call the local utility locating service for help. Be sure to check local setback regulations, too. Finally, use the wish list that you made during the initial phase of design to help you sketch deck possibilities on tracing paper until you settle on a design that works for you.

Finalizing the plan

There's a lot of detail to sort through in order to transform your rough sketch into a work-ing plan that you can submit to the building department. You'll also use your final plan to work up a materials list showing how much wood and hardware to buy.

If you're not comfortable drafting your own plan, you can hire a landscape architect, a drafting service, or a professional deck contractor. You can also take your rough plans to a home center that offers computer deck-design service. These options all produce a set of working drawings and a bill of materials.

Drawing your own deck plan

The people in the building department want to see details. You will have to work out the location of the posts, the footing depth and diameter, and the size of all framing members. The plan should also show the railings and stairway.

Most plans are drawn at ¼ scale, which means ¼ inch on the drawing equals 1 foot on the ground. Since it can be difficult to cram all the necessary information onto one page, you may find yourself using one sheet to show the pattern of the decking boards and another for the understructure. You will also need to show the deck in elevation and plan views.

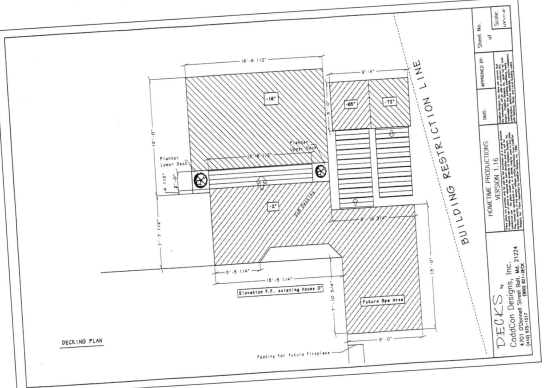

Professionally drawn plans take the guesswork out of design and get you to the building phase fast. Another option is ready-made plans, which are usually sold at home centers or through advertisements in building magazines.

Put all the important dimensions on the drawings, labeling the size and type of lumber to be used as well as any hardware shown.

Larger detail drawings and cross-sections are very helpful. While you can draw them precisely to scale, it's a lot of trouble and not really necessary, as long as you write down the correct dimensions.

When you've finished your plan, make two photocopies for the building department. Don't be alarmed if the department suggests revisions, since many can be worked out on the spot. Make the changes as suggested, then re-submit the plan.

Peel-and-stick kits

These kits come with templates that let you play around with various elements of deck design until you get it just right. They usually work on the modular system. You combine the modules to create the deck you want.

Cardboard models

Some people find that a model is the best way to visualize a big project. Paste copies of scale drawings onto cardboard or foamcore, then cut out the pieces and glue on miniature posts, railings, and steps.

Do-it-yourself computer design

Many programs allow homeowners to design a deck on the computer. A good program not only lets you view your deck from any angle, it also takes care of sizing the lumber according to code, and it should spit out an accurate materials list. However, try to talk to someone who has used the program, or arrange to try it for yourself, before you buy – software marketers often make promises they can't keep.

The computer *can present your deck design in three dimensions, a useful feature that allows you to see what the finished deck will look like.*

Scale drawings

You can draw your plans on either graph paper or plain paper using an architect's rule. This triangular ruler offers ten different scales as well as a regular 12-inch rule: the smallest representation of 1 foot is $3/32$ inch, the largest is 3 inches. Other useful drawing tools are a drafting triangle, protractor, compass, and T-square.

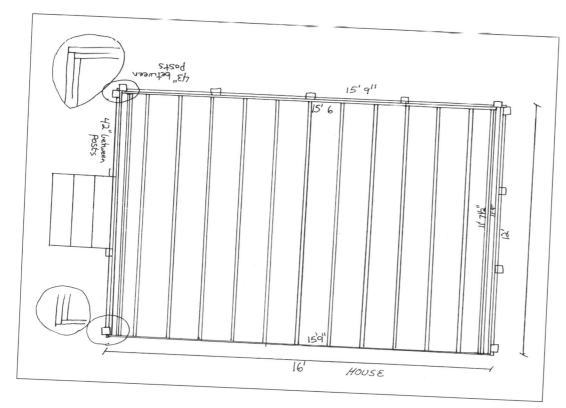

Your deck plan *doesn't need to be a work of art. Just be sure your intentions are clear. You can always write a note describing an element that you aren't sure how to draw.*

It's best to have the wood delivered a couple of weeks before you start construction so it can acclimate to local moisture conditions. Professional builders would just leave it in a bundle or stacked in a tight heap, but this is one place the homeowner can do a better job. Promote air circulation by stacking the wood in layers with 1x2 spacers in between, then cover the pile loosely with plastic to shield it from the rain. While you're stacking the lumber, set aside the boards with the straightest grain for use as railings, trim, and other highly visible parts of the deck. This staging time allows you to get familiar with what you've got, so you can use the best wood in the most visible places – a nice touch professional builders just can't afford.

Permits and Inspections

Before beginning to build, you need to obtain a building permit from your local building department, and you have to post it where it can be seen from the street.

The building inspector will visit your site at a few key stages during construction. Here the inspector checks the footing depth to make sure it complies with code.

Post building permits where they are clearly visible from the street. If you don't get a permit, you could be fined or even be told to rip out the work you've done.

Although most communities draw their codes from national standards, local modifications are often made to keep up with new materials as well as with local conditions. Even if you think you know the code, you should check with the building department before each project.

Although the building code specifies minimum construction standards, a building inspector will never penalize you for over-building. While building officials are accustomed to dealing with professionals who know what is needed to get a permit, most of them are more than willing to help you figure out what's required.

Scheduling inspections

Talk to the building inspector to find out how many inspections you'll need; for decks, it's usually just a few. Usually the inspector will come out to check the footing forms before the concrete pour, again to inspect the framing prior to installation of the decking, and then again when the deck is completed. If electrical work will be done, that will require a separate inspection, as will any spa plumbing.

The ground under the deck *should pitch away from the house at a slope of at least ¼ inch per foot to allow rainwater to run off. To check the grade, use a level on top of a 2x4, then measure from the ground to the bottom edge of the leveled board.*

Spread landscape fabric *on the ground to prevent weeds from popping through the spaces between deck boards. Overlap the edges of the fabric at least 6 inches.*

Site Preparation

Good under-deck drainage is essential because it keeps rot-producing moisture down. It also makes the area less hospitable to insects. Even under low decks, the ground should slope away from the house. If you're building on steep property, you will have to route rainwater runoff so it doesn't erode channels into the hillside. Building a deck on a steep grade can be tricky, so you may have to consult with an engineer.

Even though pachysandra and other shade-loving groundcovers usually won't grow under decks less than a story high, there are many weeds that will. A layer of landscape fabric or black plastic buried under a couple of inches of mulch or gravel will keep the weed population down. If you use plastic, make sure to punch small holes every 3 to 4 feet to allow water to escape.

Marking out utility lines

If you're not certain of the location of the buried electrical, telephone, or water lines on your property, find out where they are; you need to have them marked before you begin deck construction. Most states have free one-call services to get all utilities marked. Use them and you'll be spared from making an expensive – or perhaps even fatal – mistake.

Shovel *a 2- to 3-inch layer of gravel on top of the landscape fabric. Not only will it disguise and secure the fabric, it will ensure that the area drains properly.*

LAYOUT

During the layout stage, *you transfer the dimensions of your deck from the plans to your site. This is painstaking work because corners must be square, horizontal surfaces must be level, and vertical surfaces must be plumb. Since even tiny errors multiply quickly into major ones, check your measurements frequently. Layout starts with the ledger board – the piece of lumber that attaches your deck to the house. Make sure you level the ledger with great care, because it's the reference point for everything else.*

Start with the Ledger

Choose a straight, clear plank for the ledger. It's going to be lag-screwed or bolted to the house framing, so the first step is to remove the siding and anything else that might be in the way. Unzip vinyl or aluminum siding, or cut through wood siding.

Use your tape measure, level, and chalk line to mark the location of the ledger on the side of the house. Mark the ends of the ledger as well as its top edge, and also mark the ends of the rim joists that will butt into the side of the house.

Next, lay out the joist locations and nail the joist hangers to the ledger and end rim joist, then tack the ledger in place. Drill pilot holes and fasten the ledger to the house framing with lag screws or carriage bolts spaced 16 inches apart. Lag screws should penetrate twice the thickness of the ledger; carriage bolts go through and receive nuts and washers on the other side of the house's rim joist. To keep water from getting into the wall, be sure to caulk the fasteners and install flashing above the ledger.

Trimming wood siding

You'll have to cut away wood siding to make room for the ledger board plus the thickness of the decking. Remember to add length to accommodate the thickness of the side rim joists. Set your saw so it will cut only the siding, not the sheathing underneath. Be sure to wiggle a piece of flashing up under the siding and over the top of the ledger.

1 *Remove vinyl siding* by unlocking the strips with a zip tool. Tuck the blade under the bottom edge of the overlapping piece of siding then pull down as you slide the tool along.

2 *Draw a level line* along which to align the ledger. The ledger plus the decking board above it should be 1 to 2 inches below the level of the interior floor so water can't flow into the house.

3 *Lay out the joists* on the ledger, and transfer the marks to the end rim joist. Generally they're spaced 16 inches on center.

4 *Nail the joist hangers* to the ledger before fastening it in place. Then align the ledger to the layout line and tack it up. Drill pilot holes for pairs of 1/2-inch carriage bolts or lag screws spaced 16 inches apart.

5 **Insert the carriage bolts,** then tighten the nuts until the square shoulders are drawn into the wood. To keep from gumming up the threads, apply caulk around the bolt heads after inserting the bolts, but before seating them fully.

6 **Insert at least 2 inches** of Z-flashing up under the siding. Overlap and caulk all the seams above the ledger, but don't caulk below it or you will trap any moisture that gets in.

Construction safety

During deck construction you're liable to encounter flying wood chips, shards of metal, and masonry fragments. To protect yourself, always wear safety glasses or goggles; add ear protection when using power tools, and a particle mask when cutting pressure-treated wood.

While you should wear work gloves to handle lumber, for better control and to eliminate the risk of the tool blade or motor catching the glove fabric, most people remove them when working with power tools. Button your cuffs (or wear shirts with short sleeves), and tie your hair back if it's long.

7 **Nail the flashing high up,** one nail every 3 or 4 feet. Caulk thoroughly where the flashing passes under the door threshold.

8 **Install new J-channel** around the ledger board to anchor the edges of the vinyl siding and keep water out. Reinstall the vinyl siding pieces you originally took off, trimming them to fit around the ledger and side rim joists.

Attaching a ledger to brick or stucco

Attaching a ledger to masonry walls is not much different from attaching it to wood. Stucco, which is a coating of cement plastered onto a wood wall, is firm enough so it doesn't have to be removed. Drill pilot holes into the stucco with a ⅜-inch masonry bit. Replace the masonry bit with a ¼-inch bit and lengthen the pilot hole into the house's sheathing and rim joist. Fasten the ledger with ½-inch x 5-inch lag screws (or carriage bolts if you have access to the interior framing), then caulk both the screwheads and all the spaces between the ledger and the stucco. For brick or concrete block, drill holes then install masonry anchors.

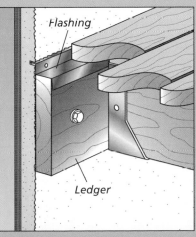

Attach the ledger directly to a stucco wall. Use a carbide-tipped masonry blade to score a line in the stucco for the top edge of Z-flashing.

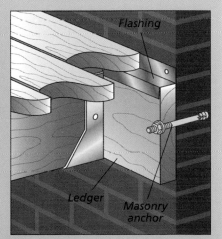

Use masonry anchors to fasten a ledger to brick or concrete block walls. Fasten the top edge of the flashing with hardened masonry nails.

1 ***Temporarily*** *screw each of the side rim joists to the ledger board. Level the rim joists and securely support them on temporary braces. Then temporarily screw the end rim joist to the side rim joists.*

Locating the Footings

There are three ways to lay out footing locations. No matter which you choose, you install the ledger board first. The ledger gives you a solid, level surface from which to make accurate layout measurements.

For simple decks, it makes the best sense to use the actual framing pieces to locate the footings. You cut the two side rim joists and the end rim joist to length, tack them together, square them up, and drop plumb lines where the posts should be. For more complicated deck designs, you can measure by putting up string lines and batter boards (see pages 44-45). The third choice, for complex, multi-level decks, is to build in stages, combining the first two approaches. First locate and install footings nearest the house, build that part of the deck, then locate the next section, using the first section for a reference. This approach requires more than one concrete pour, but it ensures that the footings end up where you want them to be.

2 ***Check*** *that the frame is perfectly square. To do this, measure both diagonals, then adjust as necessary until both diagonals measure the same.*

Shoot for square

Every phase of deck construction requires frequent checks for level and square, but these checks are especially crucial during layout. Even though your lumber may be cut to perfect length and everything looks nice and square when you eyeball it, there's no guaran-

3 ***Tack*** *diagonal braces in place to hold the framework square while you locate the posts on the ground.*

4 ***Drop a plumb bob*** *from the layout string to the ground to find the center of each post.*

tee that the assembly actually is square unless you measure it.

An easy way to check that framing members are square is to measure the diagonals and then to compare the measurements. They should be equal. If they're not, you must push and pull the framing members, and measure again. When the framing finally measures square, keep it that way by nailing a couple of diagonal braces across the corners. Although the bracing is temporary, it must be sturdy enough to prevent the framing from being knocked out of square as you work around it.

From framing to ground

Once you've determined that the assembled rim joists are square, the next task is to mark the post locations on the ground. To do this, check your plans to find out exactly how far out from the house the beam and the posts will go. With a tape, measure out from the house along the side rim joists, mark the distance by tapping in a nail on each joist, then stretch a string between the nails. Measure along the string to locate the posts according to your plan, then transfer the location of the post centers to the ground.

A plumb bob is the most accurate tool for transferring post locations. Mark the center of each post location on the ground with a 16d nail punched through a piece of tape or ribbon.

Remove the framing

Once the footings are marked, you can take down the rim joists so you'll have room to dig footing holes and pour concrete. If you're careful to mark how everything fits together, it will be quick and easy to put it all back up when you're ready.

Straight shot

In beamless construction, you don't need to use a string line and plumb bob because you can shoot right off the end rim joist to find the footings. Just use a 4-foot level and plumb down directly from the framing to locate the posts, nudging the level until the bubble indicates that it is vertical. Be sure you are marking the center of each post – remember to compensate for any notches in the posts.

Layout by Measurement

In this method of layout, you use mason's lines attached to batter boards to establish the edges and corners of the deck. Once these points and lines are determined, you can locate the posts by stretching additional strings as needed.

To get started, use a plumb bob to transfer the outside edges of the deck from the ledger board down to ground level. (With a ground-level deck, fasten the layout strings to nails tacked into the ledger board.) You'll be using mason's string and stakes or batter boards at each outside deck corner to secure the lines.

Batter boards

Batter boards give you an anchor for leveling and tying off string lines. They're simple to make from 1x2 stakes fastened to a crosspiece with drywall screws. Keep the crosspiece about 2 inches below the top edges of the stakes. For stability, pound the batter boards about 6 inches into the ground; to keep them out of the way while you're pouring the footings, locate the batter boards several feet beyond the corners of the deck. Then run mason's string out to each batter board, using a framing square to approximate square corners. Temporarily wrap the string around the batter board to secure it in place.

Finding square

You can always establish a square corner by using basic geometry: A triangle with sides in the ratio 3-4-5 (or multiples of 3-4-5, such as 6-8-10) always has a 90-degree corner. To use this formula, first locate the corner you want to make square, drive a nail into it, and tie a mason's line onto the nail. Now measure 6 feet along the ledger board, and 8 feet along the line. Then swing the line until the diagonal between the two points is exactly 10 feet long, which means that the corner is a precise right angle. When the string is square, wrap it around a nail tapped into the top of the batter board crosspiece at the proper location. Make sure to leave at least 2 inches of nail sticking up above the crosspiece so you can adjust the string to the correct height.

If the house wall is uneven – and most are – it's best to establish a straight line parallel to the house, then use that as a reference for stringing the layout lines. The line is parallel when it is the same distance from the house at several points.

To square a line to the corner of the house, tack it to the corner then adjust it so it's parallel to the reference line. If it is, it will also be square to the house.

Established reference lines can be used to locate layout lines anywhere the plan indicates there should be a line of posts. Always measure carefully so the lines remain parallel, otherwise your layout will not be square.

Marking the footings

Use a line level to make sure all your layout strings are level. If a string isn't level, raise or lower it on the nail until it is. After you've squared and leveled the two strings representing the side rim joists, measure out from the house to locate the beam (or the end rim joist, if you are using post and rim joist construction). Mark the location on each string, then tie a third string across those marks. Using your plan as a reference, measure and mark the center of each post position on the string. Line up a plumb bob with each mark on the string, drop the plumb bob to transfer those marks to ground level, then mark each spot on the ground with a nail driven through a piece of tape or ribbon.

Layout as you go

On a complex multi-level deck that wraps around the corner of the house, it might be difficult to locate all of the post locations at one time. The thing to do is be sure you have a general idea where things will go, then start with the deck section closest to the house. Attach its ledger board to the house, locate and dig the holes, pour the footings, erect the posts and attach the rim joists. Now you will be able to use the completed section as a reference to locate the next section.

To establish a perpendicular layout line, use the 3-4-5 method to square the perpendicular line to the established reference line. Measure out 3 feet along one line, and 4 feet along the adjacent line (above). Then adjust the string until the two marks are exactly 5 feet apart (left). This ensures that the two strings form a precise right angle.

Mark each post location on the string and then transfer the location to the ground with a plumb bob. Drive a 16d nail through a ribbon or piece of tape into the ground as a marker.

Footings

For stability, footings must always be set below the frost line in climates where the ground freezes in winter. Proper footing depth will vary around the country, so check with your building department before doing any digging. Also check on proper footing diameter. Call the building department to schedule an inspector to come out and check the depth and diameter of your footing holes before you pour the concrete.

Digging the holes

It's possible to dig footing holes by hand using a post-hole digger, but this can be back-breaking, time-consuming work. It's far easier to rent a power auger, although in rocky areas you may have no choice but to dig the holes manually.

When using a power auger, drill until the bit starts to slow down, then pull it up and clear out the dirt. If your footings are deeper than 36 inches, you probably will need to put an extension on the bit to reach the correct depth. The deeper you go, the harder it gets to pull up the auger high enough to clear the extension bit – a good reason to consider hiring someone else to drill the holes.

1 *A **gas-powered auger** speeds digging the footing holes and is worth renting when there are many holes to dig below the frost line. Two-operator models are easier to handle than one-operator types. Contact your local rental center to see what's available. Be sure to get instructions before leaving the store.*

Safe footing

Use scrap plywood to cover footing holes that won't be filled immediately. This will protect people and animals from stumbling into the holes, and it also keeps debris out. If you're building in cold weather, covers will also help keep the holes from freezing before you're ready to pour the concrete.

***Hiring an auger operator** to dig the holes makes sense if your deck requires many footings. A contractor can dig a dozen holes in an hour or two. Your local home center will probably be able to give you referrals.*

To make the footings as stable as possible, use a post-hole digger to bell out the bottom of the hole. If the footing is wider at the bottom, it will be harder for it to get pushed around by frost. Again, always check with your building department to find out what is required in your area.

The last step is to tamp down the bottom of the footing hole – you don't want the entire deck to be sitting on loose chunks of soil that will eventually compress and settle.

Setting the form tubes

Tube-shaped fiberboard forms let you pour concrete above ground level, which protects the post from coming into contact with soil and water. In areas with sandy or unstable soils, they may even be required by code. Typically 4x4 posts use 8-inch diameter forms; 6x6 posts use 10-inch or 12-inch forms. Again, codes will dictate diameter.

Before installing the tubes, spread 2 to 3 inches of gravel in the bottom of each hole. Cut the tube to length with a saw; it should extend 6 inches above ground level and 6 to 12 inches below. Insert the tube in the hole and spike it into the soil with nails. It's important that the tube stop short of the bottom of the hole so concrete can flow into the bell.

2 *Allow the top* of the fiberboard form to protrude a few inches above the soil. Anchor the form with nails driven through the form and into the soil. Before the pour, check the top of the form to make sure it's level.

3 *For small jobs*, mix bagged concrete with water in a mason's tray or wheelbarrow. Use a hoe to chop and turn the concrete. Mix until the concrete holds its shape when you slice it with the hoe.

4 *Shovel concrete* into the forms, making sure not to knock them around. Every now and then poke the concrete with the end of a piece of lumber to release any air pockets.

5 *Screed the concrete* level with the form using a piece of scrap lumber.

Burying the post

If the soil in your area has a high clay composition (which will allow a hole to hold its shape during digging), you can use a different type of construction. This consists of digging a hole, pouring a concrete pad below the frost line, running the post into the ground to rest on the concrete pad, then backfilling the hole with dirt. This technique requires pressure-treated posts. A level footing provides a post with solid support. Use a rake to level the concrete pad at the bottom of the footing hole.

Connecting Posts to Footings

Mechanical connections hold the posts to the footings, protecting the posts against uplift and lateral movement. In some areas they are required by code.

One common anchoring system uses metal brackets that are J-bolted to the concrete footing. Although the brackets allow some adjustment, try to get each J-bolt as close as possible to the projected center of its post.

Precast concrete pier blocks can be set into footings to support deck posts above the soil. In warm areas the blocks may be set directly on a shallow concrete pad, though this is not a good idea in areas prone to hurricanes or tornadoes.

Set J-bolts or metal post anchors into the wet concrete, being careful not to gum up the threads with concrete. Restring a line to help align the bolts and use a torpedo level to plumb them.

After the footings have cured, tear off the above-ground fiberboard and attach the anchor brackets. Align the brackets against a straight 2x4, then bolt them down.

Precast concrete pier blocks are often used to raise posts above grade. Set the blocks in the wet concrete, then level them before the concrete sets so the posts will stand solid on the surface.

Attach post anchor brackets to the pier block with special hardened screws. Predrill the block using a masonry bit.

Some concrete pier blocks have wells to hold the posts ends. This provides lateral support, but no protection against lifting in heavy wind. Because the wells collect water, use pressure-treated posts.

FRAMING

Once you've fastened the ledger board to the house *and poured footings for the posts, framing the deck is pretty straightforward. There are a few important things to remember as you go, however. You'll want to pick over your material carefully, choosing the best looking planks for visible places, and putting the other stuff underneath. When installing posts, check to see which corner is closest to square. Install that corner toward the inside of the deck, because you'll be measuring off it. When installing joists, check them for crown, and install the crowned edge upward. Pay close attention that the framing members are installed plumb and square. This will make your deck as sturdy as it is good-looking.*

Posts

The main thing to remember when setting posts is that the tops of the posts have to be level with each other, or the deck beams won't sit flat and level. Because the footings are different heights, the length of each post may vary and will need to be determined individually. The technique is the same, whether you're resting the base of the post on a footing below the frost line, or anchoring it above grade to a concrete pier. If you used fiberboard tube forms to build footings that rise above ground level, rip off the fiberboard to get it out of your way once the concrete has cured. It will make the construction look better, too.

Determining post height

If you used the rim joists to locate the posts, it's important to get the joist framework perfectly level when you reinstall it. Why? Because you'll be using the framework to determine how high the posts are. Clamp the rim joists to temporary 2x4 braces and check again that the framework is still level. Now set the first post in position and use the level to plumb it in both directions. Level across from the bottom of the rim joist to make a mark that represents the bottom of the joists. On a post and rim joist deck, this will be the height of the post. On a post and beam deck,

1 **Temporarily** set the post in its bracket, plumbing it with a level in both directions. Then mark the bottom of the rim joist on the post. Subtract the depth of the beam to establish the cut line.

2 **Trimming a 4x4 post** takes two passes of the circular saw. Cut halfway through, rotate the post, and finish the cut from the opposite side. It will be easier to follow the cut line if you extend the line around all four sides of the post. Note the mark to the left of the saw. It represents the bottom of the rim joist. From there, we measured down the depth of the beam to mark the cutting line.

Protecting post ends

Because the chemicals used to treat the lumber may not have penetrated all the way to the center of the wood, seal the cut ends of pressure-treated posts with a solution containing 2% copper preservative. This step is especially important when the cut end will be horizontal (such as the top of a post), because water is more likely to pool on horizontal surfaces.

3 *To install posts in anchor brackets*, set them in place and plumb them with a level. Tap the first nail through the bracket hole into the post to secure it in place, then check plumb again.

4 *Brace the posts* once you've gotten them plumb. Then drive the rest of the nails through the brackets into the post bottoms. Leave the braces in place until the deck framing is complete.

you'll have to measure down again by the depth of the beam.

If you're installing the posts before you build the rim joist framework, you'll have to use a 2x4 long enough to extend from the ledger board past the post. Set one end of the 2x4 in a joist hanger on the ledger board and run the other end alongside the post. Set a carpenter's level on top to make sure the 2x4 stays level. Then use a second level to check the post for plumb. Mark where the bottom of the 2x4 crosses the post. That transfers the height of the bottom of the ledger board (the bottom of the joists) to the post. If your deck design includes a beam, measure down from the mark by the depth of the beam.

Marking and cutting the posts

Use a square to draw a straight line through your marks on each post. Since a circular saw won't cut clear through a 4x post, continue the straight line to the remaining sides to create cutting lines all the way around the post.

On 4x4 posts it takes two saw cuts to trim the post. Since 6x6 posts are too big for a circular saw to cut through in two passes, you'll have to make four cuts and finish with a handsaw. When you're sawing all around a 6x6 post, you may have trouble keeping the cuts in line. You can nail scraps of 1x4 all around the post to act as a saw guide, or you can use a speed square as a guide.

Other ways to attach posts

Builders in different parts of the country tend to favor different methods for attaching posts to footings. Ask around to find out what works best in your region.

If you don't want to mess with setting J-bolts in wet concrete, drill a hole in the footing after the concrete has cured, and a mating hole in the bottom of the post. A piece of rebar inserted in the holes will hold the posts in place. Because it doesn't resist upward lift, this method is not advisable in high-wind regions.

Another method is to bed the post directly on a concrete footing at the bottom of the hole. Plumb the posts carefully, then backfill with soil. Be sure to use pressure-treated lumber for buried posts.

Before installing posts on pins, add a square of builder's felt and a squirt of caulk to keep water out of the joint.

When backfilling buried posts, tamp the soil in thin layers to compress it and to release air pockets. Check frequently for plumb – it's easy to knock the posts off plumb when tamping.

Beams

The beams rest on the posts and, together with the ledger, support the joists. There are two types of beams. A beam positioned below the joists is called a dropped beam. A beam positioned at the same level as the joists is called a flush beam.

Regardless of the type of beam, your local building code will probably require that beams be double or triple the size of the joists for proper support. You usually just sandwich two or three planks together, but you can also special-order solid beams. When assembling the beam from separate pieces of lumber, pay attention to nail length. If the nails are as long as the beam will be thick, drive them in at a slight angle so the tips won't protrude on the opposite side. You can also use ½-inch lag screws or carriage bolts to assemble the beam. On a triple 2x10 beam, the bolts should be 5 inches long to pass through all three boards.

Assemble the beam by nailing together two planks of 2x10 or 2x12 lumber that have been cut to length. Drive three 10d nails every 16 inches on center along the full length of the planks.

Adjust the beam under the rim joist structure. Prop up the rim joists with shims to allow the beam to fit underneath and to make it easier to position.

Fasten the beam to the post. The hardware you use will depend on the size of the posts and beam. With this deck, the hardware consists of pairs of brackets that slip in under the beam from each side and are then nailed in place with galvanized joist-hanger nails.

Beam splices

Even if you can find them, long planks that will create beams to span the full length of your deck may be expensive. Beams spliced together out of shorter lengths of lumber will not only be cheaper, they'll also be easier to handle, because you can raise sections of the beam, then fasten them together once they're in place. If you install spliced beams properly, they're every bit as strong as beams made of full-length planks.

When installing a spliced beam, remember that the splice itself must be supported directly by a post underneath. Generally, at least an inch of each end of a spliced beam should bear on the post. Otherwise, the connection may fail. In addition, reinforce both sides of the splice with either a steel T-connector or a wooden gusset plate nailed or screwed into the beam.

Notched posts

Occasionally posts will have to be notched to accommodate a beam, especially if the posts run up past the deck to form part of the railing or a built-in bench. Don't notch more than half-way into a post that continues upward past the notch or you will seriously weaken it. Before assembling the joint, it's a good idea to apply a wood preservative containing at least 2% copper to the horizontal part of the notch to protect it from rotting.

To cut a notch in the end of a post, first score the outline of the cut with a circular saw, then finish with a handsaw and chisel. Predrill holes for lag screws before putting the post in place.

Corner posts can be notched from two adjacent sides, so they can support intersecting joists. The tenon that remains helps locate the post, but since the post does not continue upward, the tenon is not structural.

Seat the beam in the notch of the post. Temporarily toenail the assembly to keep it stable, then, after the last couple of joists are in, attach the beam permanently with lag screws.

Bolted beams

Deck plans often show a two-piece beam sandwiching a post, held with a ½-inch bolt through all three pieces. This makes it easy to extend the post upward to support a railing, a built-in bench, or an overhead structure.

However, bolting the beam planks directly to the post may not pass code in your area; it doesn't make a strong connection because the load is transferred to the bolt instead of the post.

If you must use a sandwich beam, use one of these methods to strengthen the joint: cut a notch in each side of the post to support the beam pieces, use a special metal bracket made for attaching a beam to the side of a post, or lag-screw wood cleats underneath the beam.

Checking for crown

Joist lumber is almost never perfectly straight – there is usually some bow toward one edge; this is known as crown.

Before installing the joists, check each one by sighting down the edge. Make a mark on the edge that is crowned, then make sure to install the crowned edge upward. This way the joists will all start off slightly high in the center and will slowly sag back toward level as the deck ages.

Joists

After installing the beams and rim joists and squaring up the structure, measure the interior, or field, joists, cut them to length, and set them in place. Plan the order of installation of the joists before you start nailing, so you know there will always be room to swing the hammer.

If joists are stubborn about sliding down into the joist hangers, tap them with a hammer to push them down and in. If a joist is tight against the beam or ledger board, however, cut a little off the end to make it fit. Don't force a long joist in – that could push the posts out of plumb or distort the end rim joist.

1 *Double the rim joists* and interweave the ends to strengthen the corners. An inside corner bracket provides even more security, while a hurricane strap ties the side rim joist to the beam.

2 *Install the field joists* so that they run perfectly straight between the ledger board and the end rim joist. To keep everything aligned, nail the joist hangers on 16-inch centers before you attach the ledger board and end rim joist.

3 *Drive nails* through the end rim joist into the ends of the field joists. Use two nails per joist.

4 *To check that* the end rim joist is straight, tie a line across the end of the deck and use a spacer block to make sure the gap is even all along the rim joist.

Splicing joists

You can't always find planks long enough to span the complete deck. While joists can be spliced, the splices must fall over a beam. Consequently the decision to splice has to be made while planning, not in the middle of the project – this isn't a decision to make on the fly. One way to make the splice is by overlapping the joists on top of the beam. Make the overlap 12 inches long, and nail the lap together. The other way is to butt the joists end to end over the support beam, and to reinforce the splice with a steel splice plate.

Decking patterns

Keep in mind that the decking pattern you choose will affect the construction of the understructure of your deck. Diagonal, chevron, picture-framed, and basket weave decking patterns all require different underpinnings for proper support. A basket weave pattern requires that the joists be built as modules – actually, as a series of mini-decks. Doubled joists and blocking are usually required wherever the decking changes direction.

Install rail posts inside the joists now

Many deck designs call for railing posts to be a continuation of the deck posts. Others call for separate railing posts to be bolted to the inside or outside of the rim joists. If your posts need to be bolted to the inner face of the rim joists, install them now, because once the decking goes on, you won't be able to attach them.

5 *Adjust the field joists* as necessary to move the end rim joist in or out. It's okay to have a small gap between the ledger board and the joist – it helps keep water from being trapped in the joint.

6 *Use hurricane and seismic anchors* to ensure that joists won't lift off the beams in the worst weather conditions. In some areas they're required by code.

7 *Attach the second end rim joist* last. It will cover all the nail heads on the ends of the joists and add strength and rigidity to the framework.

8 *Plane down* any joist end that is higher than the adjoining rim joist. Otherwise, it will push up the deck boards and make them rock.

Temporary posts support the framework until everything is set and the permanent posts are placed. Run diagonal braces to stakes to make sure the temporary posts stay put.

1 *The side rim joist* rests on a temporary cleat screwed into the ledger board. The cleat supports one end of the rim joist while a temporary post is installed at the other. An inside corner bracket makes the final connection between rim joist and ledger.

2 *Brace temporary posts* with 2x4s. This will ensure that the structure stays level and square while you complete the framing and install the beam and permanent posts.

Framing Down

It used to be that raised decks were built from the ground up. First the posts were installed, then the beams were installed, followed by the rim joists. Unfortunately, even if you measured carefully when locating the footings and posts, it wasn't uncommon to find that one or more posts was slightly out of position when it came time to frame the substructure. But for some time now, contractors have been building decks from the joists down, which makes it easier to locate the footings and posts exactly where they belong.

Maneuvering joists and beams up in the air without posts to rest them on is not easy, and you probably won't be able to do it alone. The work goes quickly with two people, though, and pieces of wood that have to be supported in mid-air can be braced with cleats and temporary posts.

Construction begins at the ledger board, with the side rim joists, but instead of using permanent posts to brace the structure, you use temporary posts. Although you could use conventional construction techniques (laying out, cutting, and placing the permanent posts

3 *Screw a small* wood cleat to the bottom edge of the side rim joist. This will support the end rim joist while you position it and nail it in place.

4 ***Level each framing member*** *as you install it. Since the placement of each framing member affects all the others, it's important to stay on track.*

5 ***Position the end rim joist*** *on the support cleat screwed to the side rim joist. The long cleat shown here will temporarily support a beam for the next level of the deck.*

first), it's faster and more accurate on a raised deck to use temporary 2x4 posts to support the framework until everything is just the way you want it. At that point, you can install the permanent posts and remove the temporary ones.

It's best to position the field joists in their hangers and hold them temporarily in place with a toenail in

each. Then adjust the position of the field joists to make sure the end rim joist remains straight. To square the deck, measure the diagonals and push the framework one way or the other until the diagonals are equal. If the deck's shape follows a bump-out, you can square up the corners using the 3-4-5 method.

Make sure the deck is level (if it's not, make adjustments to the temporary posts until it is), then position the beam under the framework using temporary cleats to hold it in position. Now you can measure down from the bottom of the beam to the top of each footing to get the exact height for each permanent post.

6 ***Nail the end rim joist*** *to the side rim joists. Next, install some – but not all – of the field joists. You just need a few to make the platform more rigid and less likely to be knocked out of square as you install the beam.*

7 ***To determine*** *the height of the posts, measure down from the bottom of the beam to the top of the footing. Cut each post to the correct height with a circular saw, and treat the horizontal cut surface with 2% copper solution.*

Permanent Post Bracing

Any deck extending farther than 16 feet from the house should be braced unless it is on grade. In addition, most raised decks require bracing – check with your local building department to find out the specific requirements for your area. Lateral bracing should always be incorporated to support decks in areas prone to high winds or earthquakes. If your deck will support unusually heavy loads, such as the weight of a spa or snow, bracing is also a must.

While knee-bracing deck posts allows more usable space underneath a raised deck, it's generally recommended that the outside posts on decks more than 8 feet high have some sort of cross-bracing. For distances measuring less than 8 feet, you can use 2x4 braces; greater distances demand 2x6 bracing. It's easier to cut braces for tall posts if you measure them in place and then cut them on the ground. Bolts or lag screws are good for fastening bracing to deck posts. Make sure to allow a small gap in the joint where braces meet to allow water to drain through. For protection against moisture damage and rot, coat the braces with wood preservative and also squirt a shot of caulk into the fastener holes.

X-bracing is symmetrical and strong, too. Install a block where the braces cross, then bolt the braces together through the block.

Y-bracing, or knee-bracing, is lighter-looking than other bracing designs, but not as sturdy as full-length bracing. It is strongest when the braces meet at a 90-degree angle.

Diagonal bracing is more effective if you add a horizontal brace that's fastened to each post with lag screws or carriage bolts.

Corner bracing should run up from the post at a 45-degree angle. If you attach the bracing inside the rim joist and butt it against the post, strengthen the connection to the post with an inside corner bracket.

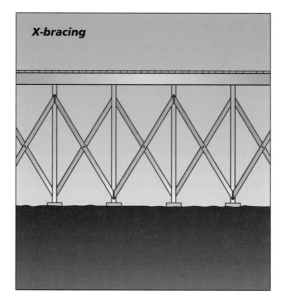

X-bracing

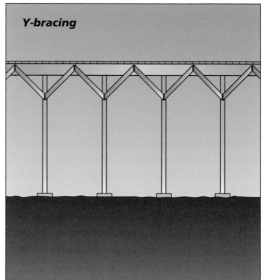

Y-bracing

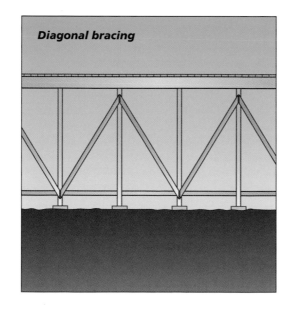

Diagonal bracing

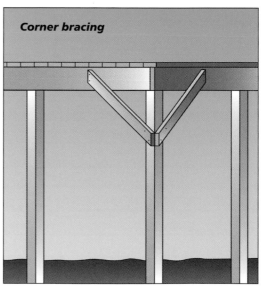

Corner bracing

DECKING

The decking is the most visible feature of the deck. It's important to install it carefully because it stiffens up the whole structure, and it also takes the most abuse from traffic and weather. Neatness, straightness, and consistent spacing are what count here. Decking is the turning point – now you will see a lot of progress in just a few hours. And once the decking is down, you'll have a place to stand while you finish the rest of your deck.

Decking

Depending on the look you want, deck boards can be 2x4s , 2x6s, or 5/4x6s. When shopping for deck boards, try to get the straightest pieces possible. If your deck isn't too wide, buy some long boards that span full width so you don't wind up with a lot of end-to-end joints.

Most of the time, you install the first decking board on the house side of the deck. It should fit close to the sheathing but not tight against it – you have to leave just enough space to allow water to drain from behind so the board won't rot out. In some situations, it's best to start the decking at the far side of the deck, so you can hide the ripped-to-width boards against the house.

Cut the two rows of boards near the house to exact length before you nail them down, because you won't have room to trim them with a circular saw later on. To get the length of the first two boards, measure from the outside edge of one rim joist to the outside edge of the opposite rim joist, then add length as needed to cover skirt boards or create any overhang you want. Let the rest of the decking boards run long over the rim joists, then trim them all at once after all the decking is installed. Working this way not only saves time, it ensures that all the boards are trimmed to a straight, even edge.

Fasteners and spacing

It's preferable to use deck screws to fasten the deck boards to the joists, but nails are okay, too. Fasteners should be long enough to penetrate the thickness of the deck boards plus 1 inch. Always use stainless steel or hot-dipped galvanized fasteners so they won't rust out. Although stainless steel or galvanized screws and nails aren't required for wood-plastic composite decking products, they're often recommended by the manufacturer. If you plan to use nails, spiral- or ring-shanked nails will hold better than regular straight nails.

Drive decking screws just flush with the surface of the deck boards – don't countersink them. Countersinking creates small pockets where water could pool. Use a drill-drive bit to help prevent stripped or broken screws. If a screw happens to break, pull the head with needle-nosed pliers and drive a second screw nearby.

For most decking materials, the typical pattern is two fasteners per board at each joist. For redwood, however, the recommendation is one fastener per board at each joist, with the fastener toward one edge on the first joist, and toward the other edge on the next.

Allow a gap between deck boards so water can drain off. Ideally, the gap should be ⅛ inch to ³⁄₁₆ inch wide. If the boards are wet when you install them (as pressure-treated lumber typically is), butt them close together without any gap. As the wood dries and shrinks, a gap will open.

It's important to avoid creating cracks or splits in the wood, especially at the ends of the boards; cracks allow water to enter, which causes rot. Drill pilot holes at the ends of the boards for both nails and screws.

Straightening bowed boards

If you have a few deck boards that are not perfectly straight, you'll probably still be able to use them. Boards that are only slightly curved should be positioned so that the curve bends away from previously installed boards. This way, one person can push the far end in while the other person fastens it in place.

If one end of the board is straight and one is curved, fasten the straight end to the joists

Secure the deck boards with two screws (or nails) where each board crosses a joist. At the board ends, drill pilot holes to avoid splitting the wood and drive the fasteners at an angle to increase their holding power.

Quick decking spacers

To create even gaps between deck boards, you can use 8d or 10d nails as spacers. Just start the spacer nail into the joist, tight against the installed board, and butt the new board against it. This will produce a gap of about ⅛ inch. Be sure to step back every now and then to look at what you are doing. Even when you use spacers it's easy to get out of whack, since boards of the same size may vary in width.

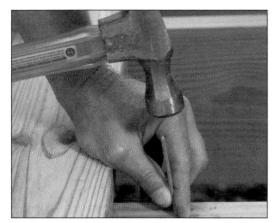

Some carpenters like to blunt the points of their nails with a hammer before nailing the board ends. This way the nails won't split or crack the wood when pounded home.

and lever the board into place with a pry bar, a wedge and brace, a chisel, or a pipe clamp. To straighten long boards, you may have to work in sections, straightening and securing one area at a time. If you're working alone, a board bender (a specialized pry-bar designed for straightening deck boards) can also come in handy. This tool lets you push the deck boards into position one-handed, leaving the other hand free for driving fasteners.

Pulling a nail

When you have to pull out a bent nail, place a small piece of scrap wood under the hammer head. This will improve your pulling

leverage and prevent the hammer head from marring the decking. To remove nails that are deeply embedded, use a nail puller; you'll get more leverage with this tool than with a claw hammer.

Some decking fasteners allow the decking to be attached without visible nails or screws. In the system shown here, you nail angled metal strips to the joists before the decking goes down. For even easier installation, install the metal strips before hanging the joists.

Complete the installation by screwing up into the deck boards from underneath. It's awkward to do this from the top side, so work from underneath if there's room.

Clips are another way to attach deck boards to the joists. You blind-nail one edge of each board into the joists, attach a small clip to the edge of the next board, then slip the clips under the edge of the first board.

One way to straighten a curved board that can't be pushed into place by hand is to fasten the straighter end of the board in place, then drive a pry bar into the joist and use it to lever the board.

Checking the layout

After installing every 6 to 8 feet of decking, it's a good idea to check that the boards are parallel. To do this, measure down to the front of the deck from both ends of the last board. Also take a measurement in the middle of the deck. If these measurements are equal, then the boards will line up straight at the end. If they're not equal, you'll have to make up the difference over the next few boards. To do this, increase the gaps between the boards slightly on the shorter side and decrease them slightly on the longer side. Then measure again so you don't go too far.

When you're about 6 feet away from the end of the deck, lay out the remaining boards to make sure you won't be left with less than half a board at the end. If necessary, take up the slack by adjusting the gap between boards. You can also rip a 2x6 to fill in a less-than-full space, or insert a 2x4.

Trimming the deck boards

The final step in decking is trimming the boards to their final length. Snap a chalk line and make a clean, straight cut with a circular saw. Use a handsaw or a jig saw to trim where a circular saw can't reach. Round off the sharp edges with a hand plane, a sanding block, a router with a roundover bit, or a Surform rasp.

Notch deck boards to fit snugly around posts mounted inside the rim joists. To mark the deck board, hold it up to the post and transfer the post's width with a square. Then cut the notch with a jig saw or handsaw.

After fastening the decking to the joists, use a framing square to transfer the location of the rim joist. Snap a chalk line from the mark down to the ends of the cut boards near the house wall.

Check your fasteners

The last step in installing the decking is to check that all fasteners are flush with the surface of the decking. Be thorough – protruding nails or screw heads will take their toll on bare feet.

Trim the deck boards to the chalk line with a circular saw. For help making a straight cut, tack a long piece of 1x4 to the deck to serve as a guide.

Diagonal Decking

In all variations of this popular decking pattern, the decking is installed at a 45-degree angle to the joists. Since some diagonal decking patterns (such as herringbone) may require building extra support into the understructure, you shouldn't change your decking from straight to a diagonal pattern at the last minute. Also, because you have to cut a 45-degree angle on each end of all the deck boards, diagonal decking creates more wood waste (about 10 percent) so you'll need to order more lumber than with straight decking patterns.

Pre-miter the board ends that go against the house to a 45-degree angle using a speed square as a cutting guide. You can make the job go even faster – and improve accuracy – by cutting the angles with a power miter saw instead of with a circular saw. Just make sure that the blade of the saw is big enough to cut through your decking boards in one shot. As with any decking, let the board ends run long over the rim joists. To save time and to ensure a perfectly straight edge, you'll trim these ends later on.

When installing diagonal decking, start in the middle and work out to the edges, filling in the spaces with courses of shorter and shorter boards. Don't fasten the deck board directly to the ledger board on the house side, because this could pierce the flashing. Instead, nail wood blocking between the joists and fasten the deck boards to the blocking. Leave enough space between the blocking and the ledger for rainwater to drip through. As you near the corners, start adjusting the board spacing so you don't wind up with tiny triangles of wood filling in the corners. Also make sure the deck boards don't drift off the 45-degree angle you've established; check frequently during installation, and adjust the board spacing as required.

Don't fasten the deck boards into the side rim joist until an entire section is installed and trimmed to length. Then check if the side rim joist is flush with the ends of the boards. If it's not, you can make minor adjustments to the side rim joist before fastening down the board ends.

For a perfect 45-degree angle, measure from the house corner of the deck to the outside corner, then measure that same distance from the outside corner along the end rim joist. Snap a chalk line between the points.

Align the board to the chalk line and fasten it down. Drive two fasteners into each joist, just as you would for perpendicular decking.

Put those scraps to work

If you stop every now and then to trim the decking boards to length, you will collect a heap of pre-mitered pieces. These come in handy when it's time to fill in the corners.

Installing the fascia

Depending on the deck design, the fascia, or skirt board, can cover just the rim joists, or it can cover the rim joists plus the ends of the deck boards. Sometimes fascia is installed before you build the stairs and railings, sometimes afterward – again, it depends on the deck design. In some situations (such as in a picture-frame deck), the frame pieces cover the cut ends of the deck boards and no fascia is needed.

Although fascia boards are usually mitered at the corners, you can also use a butt joint to connect the pieces. You can make fascia boards of 2x lumber, but you'll need material one increment wider than the joists (2x8 joists call for 2x10 fascia). Since the fascia isn't structural, you can use thinner material, such as 1x cedar, redwood, or pine. Cedar and redwood are good choices because they're naturally rot-resistant and they really dress up a deck, but pine's okay if you paint a water-repellent on all sides before installation.

Fit the fascia on the rim joist between the railing support posts. This fascia butts under the overhanging decking.

Miter the fascia so it flows around angled corners. This fascia covers the cut ends of the decking.

This two-part, stepped fascia starts with 2x8s cut to fit between rail posts. A rabbet is cut along the back of the bottom edge so the lower section of fascia will tuck tightly behind it.

The lower section is a 1x6, notched to fit around the base of the posts. Because the lower section fits behind the upper section, no gaps will be revealed as the fascia boards dry and contract.

STAIRS and RAILINGS

Stairs and railings are the finishing touches *for every deck-building project. The way you detail them has a lot to do with how well your deck project ties in with the style of your house. While stairs look complicated and require precise measurements, they're not beyond the reach of the handy homeowner. If possible, build a simple stair to a low deck to gain some experience before you tackle a complex stair with a landing.*

Simple Staircase

A staircase consists of stringers, or jacks, which support the treads. It's critical that each step in a flight be the same height, or rise, and also the same depth, or run. This means you have to figure the rise and run for the entire set of steps, then divide it so each step comes out the same. The building code specifies that the rise of each step should not exceed 8 inches, and stair builders figure that the rise plus the run should total somewhere between 17 and 21 inches (ideally, 19 inches). Some builders prefer lower steps with a rise of about 6 inches, and a combined rise and run of 17 inches for decks and other outdoor projects.

Set the landing

In order to lay out your steps, you need a fixed reference point at the top and bottom from which to measure. Use a 6-inch rise and an 11-inch run to make a rough sketch, which will help you figure out where to lo-

1 *Stairs need a solid base*, but it doesn't have to be deep. Patio blocks set in a bed of gravel or coarse sand will work, as will a pad of concrete poured in a wooden form.

cate the base pad. Cut through the turf and make a shallow concrete landing pad for the base of the steps. Make the landing level and at least six inches wider than the steps.

Calculate the rise and run

With the landing established, you can measure the total rise and run of the flight. Extend a long 2x4 off the top of the deck, measure out the total run of the steps, then measure down to the landing to find the total rise. If you make each tread with two 2x6s, the run will be about 11 inches, which most people find comfortable.

For a rise of 6 inches per step, divide the total rise by that number. If it works out even, perfect, but it probably won't. What this trial division does tell you is how many rises there will be in the total flight: round up or down to the nearest whole number. Now divide the total rise again by that whole number to find the exact rise of each step. Finally, to check the calculation, add the rise of one step to the run of the tread. If the answer is about 17 inches, you've got the rise figured right. If it's not, add or subtract a step and divide again.

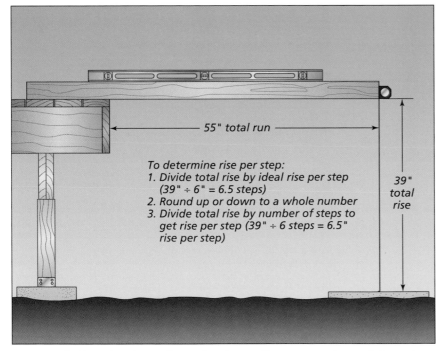

— 55" total run —

To determine rise per step:
1. Divide total rise by ideal rise per step (39" ÷ 6" = 6.5 steps)
2. Round up or down to a whole number
3. Divide total rise by number of steps to get rise per step (39" ÷ 6 steps = 6.5" rise per step)

39" total rise

2 *To calculate the rise and run* of each step, first measure the total rise and run of the flight of steps, taking into account any slope to the base pad. Choose a tread depth, 11 inches for example, and subtract it from 17 inches, leaving a target rise of 6 inches per tread. Divide the total rise by 6, then round the answer up or down to find the number of steps. Divide the total rise by this number to find the exact rise per step.

Make the stringer

Make the notched stringers out of 2x12 planks. Find the rise on the outside of one blade of the framing square and the run on the outside of the other blade, and set these two marks on the edge of the 2x12. You can buy small brass fittings called stair buttons to hold these settings. Trace the framing square to mark the shape of one step, and repeat the process until you've drawn all the steps on the board.

At the top of the stringer, extend the line for the first rise down to the bottom edge of the stringer; this will create the vertical surface that rests against the rim joist. At the other end of the stringer, extend the last run line across to the bottom edge of the stringer to create the horizontal surface that rests on the base. In order for the bottom riser to end up at the same height as the others after the treads are added, you have to cut the thickness of one tread from the bottom edge of the bottom riser. Finally, mark cutouts for braces at the top and bottom.

Check your work by sawing the plumb cut at the top and the horizontal cut at the bottom of the stringer, then hold it in position against the rim joist and base before you saw any tread notches. If it's wrong, you'll be able to adjust the layout.

You can't saw right into an inside corner with a circular saw, because of the shape of the blade. Saw as close as you can, then finish the cut with a handsaw. Saw out the notches for the stringer braces, too. Steps over 3 feet wide will need three stringers, but you only need to lay out one of them. Then, after you've cut it and checked that it fits, use it for a template to mark the other two.

Build the carriage

After you've cut all the stringers, lay them out on the deck and screw the braces to them. The braces tie the stringers into a single unit called the carriage. On stringers longer than 5 feet, add a third brace across the back of the stringers. You don't need to make notches for it.

The braces aren't needed to connect the parts of the carriage because the treads will do that job. But without bracing, you will

3 *Lay out the stringer* with a framing square. Position the square so it marks the rise of a step on one blade, and the run of a step on the other blade. In this example, the rise is 6½ inches and the run is 11 inches.

4 *Cut out the step notches* with a circular saw, then finish the inside corners with a handsaw.

5 *Once you've made* one stringer, you can use it as a template to lay out the others. Most flights require three stringers.

6 *Assemble the stair carriage* by screwing braces, or backers, to the stringers. The wide backer on the left will be used to fasten the carriage to the rim joist of the deck.

7 *In most situations* the rim joist won't be deep enough to fully support the stair carriage, so you need to add a header to it. Attach the header by nailing gusset plates on both the front and back sides.

8 *The gussets will prevent* the backer from seating flat against the rim joist and stair header if you don't mark their location and chisel out spaces for them.

have to add joist hangers to connect the stringers to the header, and you'll have to measure very carefully to get them at the same height.

Install the header

Since the rim joist forms the top riser, only part of the carriage rests against it. To fully support the carriage, you have to make the rim joist deeper with a stringer beam, or header. Nail two 2x6 planks together to make the beam, then nail it beneath the rim joist using three galvanized gusset plates on each side of the joint. Saw and chisel shallow notches in the back of the top stringer brace for the gussets so the brace will sit tight against the stringer beam.

9 *Set the carriage* in position and screw the backer to the rim joist and stringer header. Drive one screw, then check for level and plumb before driving the rest.

Install the carriage

Lift the completed carriage into position and make sure it's level. Check to be sure that the top step is the correct distance down from the deck surface: the rise of one step plus the thickness of one tread. Then screw the carriage to the rim joist and stringer header. Make sure the screws don't hang up on the metal gusset plates.

Make the treads

Before you install the treads, paint 2% copper preservative solution onto the horizontal cut surfaces of the stringers. Cut the 2x6 treads to length and fit them in place, leaving a space the thickness of a 16d nail between the boards. Screw them to the stringers with two screws at each intersection. The front of each tread should overhang the stringer by about ¼ inch to ½ inch, forming a small nosing. The nosing disguises any variation in the width of the planks or in the stringer cuts.

Skirt boards

To give the stairs a finished look, install either risers or skirt boards, but not both. Installing both on an outdoor stair makes it too hard to chase leaves and snow out of the corners of the steps. Risers go on before you install treads, skirt boards go on after the treads, but before the railings.

Make skirt boards from the same size lumber used for the stringers. Use a cut stringer as a template for marking the angled cuts at the top and bottom of the skirt board.

10 *Brush wood preservative* on the horizontal surfaces of the stringers, then screw the treads in place. An overhang at the front of the tread is called the nosing.

Alternatives to notched stringers

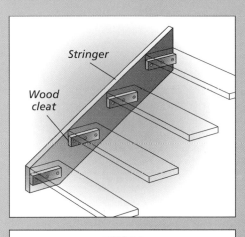

Wood cleats *screwed to solid stringers will support the treads. Use this alternative for short, narrow flights, or else you'll have to add a notched center stringer.*

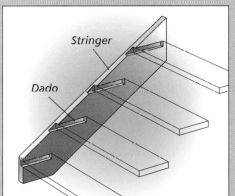

Metal cleats *work the same way as wooden ones. To locate the cleats, lay out the stringer as if you were going to saw notches.*

Dadoes, or housings, *cut into the face of the stringers make a neat stair. The dadoes can be roughed out with a circular saw and cleaned up with a chisel, or they can be routed.*

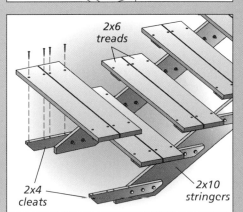

For a contemporary look, *construct cantilevered stringers by bolting 2x4 cleats onto planks. This method works best with wide steps that aren't too steep.*

Stairs with a landing look complex (and they are), but the construction can be broken down into three components: simple step, small platform deck, simple step. The difficult part is keeping all the parts square, level and at the right height, in this situation best done by building from the top down.

1 *Lift the upper carriage* into position. Tack a cleat to the rim joist ahead of time to help you position the carriage.

2 *Prop the stair carriage* with temporary 2x4 posts. Adjust the posts to level the carriage.

Stairs with a Landing

A landing is a platform that interrupts a flight of stairs – in effect, it is a very deep step, with one flight going down from it and another continuing upward from it. A landing not only improves the look of a long flight, it also allows the steps to turn, either 90 degrees or a full 180 degrees. Turning the steps at a landing allows the stairs to rise within a smaller amount of ground space, and it also permits you to control the direction from which people approach the steps. While the landing often falls in the precise middle of the flight, it doesn't have to, depending on the situation and what you are trying to accomplish.

Locating the landing

This is a tough thing to figure out because the landing has to be in exactly the right place, or else the rise and run of the steps won't work out evenly. It's essential to make accurate plan and elevation drawings on paper, and to measure often, or you can plan on cutting at least one of the stringers more than once.

To begin, locate the top and bottom of the flight. The initial location of the bottom of the flight will be approximate, but it's necessary to know about where the last step will reach the ground, or you'll be guessing about the actual height. First drop a plumb line from the upper deck to the ground immediately below and measure that distance. Next extend a level 2x4 from ground level under the deck to where the stairs will land and measure any drop in grade. Add the two measurements to find the total rise of the flight. Once you know the total rise, you can calculate the rise of the individual steps, which allows you to determine the finished

3 *Screw the backer* to the header at the top of the stairs.

height of the landing. Run lines from stakes and batter boards to locate the edges of the landing and of both flights of steps, and measure their total runs.

Building the landing

Armed with this information, you can construct the landing just as if it was a small deck. However, it's best to leave yourself a little maneuvering room. Do this by making the landing as a platform set on beams and posts. Locate and set posts and bridge them with beams. Frame up and deck the platform and tack it in place over the beams, but don't fasten it down tight just yet. If necessary, you can shift it an inch one way or the other, and you can even shim it up an inch or two.

Attaching the stringers

Now it's possible to frame stringers up from the rim joist of the landing platform to the upper deck. Lay out the bottom of the stringer so it rests on the finished surface of the landing, same as it would on a base pad. Hold the stringer in position. You may have to adjust the position of the landing platform before everything lines up correctly. When it's right, you can fasten the landing platform to its support structure, then mount the carriage for the upper stairway on it. Finally, frame the lower stair up to the platform.

To make a landing that incorporates a broad step, build the platform as described above. Then frame up the step as a second box directly on top of the landing platform. While there are other ways of making a landing with a step in it, this is the simplest.

Framing down

It's possible you'll find yourself in a situation where the only fixed point of reference is the upper deck (as with the stairway shown here). In that case, you may have no choice but to frame up the upper stair on temporary posts so you can use it as a reference for locating the landing. This is a difficult way to build a stairway, but it is one sure way to get the landing in exactly the right position.

After figuring the rise and run for the entire staircase, assemble the upper carriage. To install it, drive screws through the stringer backer into the header. Support the bottom of the carriage on temporary posts until the landing is positioned. The carriage will be heavy and awkward to maneuver, so round up some extra help.

Next lay out the header and end rim joists for the landing platform. Fasten the joist hangers on 16-inch centers, then double up the rim joists. Because the landing featured here has a step in it, an extra set of rim joists is toenailed above the lower ones. A doubled field joist strengthens the structure at the level change.

Screw the header joist to the upper carriage and support it with temporary posts. Then nail together the rest of the rim joist assembly and nail it to the header joist. Level the landing platform and brace it up on temporary posts. Install the field joists, then check that the platform is still level before measuring down to the footings to determine the height of the permanent posts. Once the permanent posts are installed, you can frame up and install the lower carriage, attach the risers, and nail down the decking and treads.

4 *Assemble* the header and end rim joists for the landing. This landing incorporates a step, so it has a double header. Drill bolt holes and attach the joist hangers before installing the headers.

5 *Bolt the header joist* to the bottom of the stair carriage. Leave the bolts loose while you level the header joist and screw it to temporary posts. Then tighten the bolts.

6 **Use the header joist** as a reference for installing the side rim joists and end rim joist. Level the assembly and support it with temporary posts. Note that all the rim joists are doubled.

7 **Drop the field joists** into the joist hangers and nail them in place. Check again that the landing frame is level and square.

8 **Measure down** from the bottom of the rim joist to the top of the footing to find the height of the landing posts. Position the posts and plumb them before securing them to the footings.

Building a ramp

The easiest way to build a ramp is to make a series of modular decks supported by posts. The posts can rest on regular footings, or they can sit on pads on the ground.

The ramp should slope no more than an inch per foot. It should be at least 36 inches wide inside the railings, with 48-inch landings at the turns. Make a 5-foot landing at the top.

Bolt modular platforms to the posts. Tilt the modules to make the slope, and fill any spaces with shims.

Screw the deck boards to the platform joists, making a smooth transition from one platform to the next.

Attach the rails to the posts, then fill in with spindles.

9 **Nail the risers** to the stringers before you attach the treads. While risers aren't strictly necessary, they do make a more finished-looking stair.

Railings

Any deck that's more than 30 inches off the ground needs a railing. In most areas, code specifies the height of deck railings (3 feet), as well as the allowable spacing (4 inches) between spindles, or balusters.

Install the posts

The first step is to install 4x4 posts about 4 feet apart – the exact spacing is up to you. Divide the total span into equal increments. You may have to fudge the spacing in order to attach the posts to the end rim joists between field joists. Notched posts that fit over the rim joist or decking are stronger than posts mounted flush with the rim joist. The posts can fit on the outside of the rim, with the notch resting on top of the deck boards, or they can be mounted inside the rim, before you install the decking (which will have to be notched to fit around the posts).

Cut the posts to length and lay out the notch, which should go half-way through the thickness. Set the saw to half the post thickness to cut the top of the notch, then set the

saw as deep as it can go and make the two lengthwise cuts. You'll have to finish the cut with a handsaw. To finish the post, bevel the bottom of the post to 45 degrees and drill two ³⁄₈-inch holes for carriage bolts. Brush 2% copper preservative solution on all of the cut surfaces.

Clamp the post in position on the rim joist

__To make a neat transition__ to the rim joist, saw a 45-degree bevel on the bottom ends of the posts.

__Clamp the post__ in place and drill holes for two ³⁄₈-inch carriage bolts.

__Cut the top railing__ to fit between the posts, screw the spindles to it, and install it. Then secure the railing by screwing the bottom of the spindles to the rim joist. Use a spacer block to keep the spindles plumb.

2x4 post gauge

If you decide to use straight posts without a notch, you'll soon find out that it's tough to install them all at the same height. The solution is to tack a 2x4 gauge piece to the back of each post before you install it. Set the end of the 2x4 onto the rim or deck, same as you would a notch. Screw or bolt the post to the rim, then remove the 2x4 gauge and go on to the next post.

Miter the cap rail and screw it to the top of the posts. The miters will stay tight together if you drive screws through the outside corner from both directions.

Anchor the cap rail with metal brackets screwed to the top of the posts. These rail clips attach from below, so there aren't any visible screw heads.

and make sure it's plumb. Use the drill to transfer the location of the bolt holes to the rim joist, then remove the post so you can drill the holes through the rim. Now squeeze a bead of construction adhesive onto the wood and bolt the post in place.

Simple spindles

The simplest way to make a railing is to cut a 2x4 so it fits exactly between the posts. Position it between the posts, on edge, flush with the post tops. Make the outside of the 2x4 flush with the outside of the rim joist, and secure it with a couple of screws at each end.

Cut the spindles so they'll reach from the bottom of the rim joist to the top of the 2x4, and bevel the bottom end to 45 degrees. Measure and evenly divide the space between the posts so that the spindles will be 4 inches or less apart. Fasten the spindles on the layout lines with one screw into the 2x4 at the top, and two screws into the rim joist at the bottom; predrill the screw holes so the wood doesn't split. Complete the railing by screwing a 2x6 cap rail on top of the posts.

Splice cap rail sections by sawing the ends at a 22½-degree angle. Drive screws at an angle through both sections and into the top of a post.

Notch cap rail sections to fit around posts that continue upward to support screens or overhead structures. Drill pilot holes and screw through the sides of the notch into the post.

Railing panels

You can't easily sweep leaves or shovel snow off a deck when the spindles go all the way down to the rim joist. The answer is a railing panel. These have top and bottom rails, with a gap between the bottom rail and the decking. To make railings with both a top and bottom rail, build them as panels or sections. Begin by cutting two pieces of 2x2 so they fit exactly between a pair of posts. These will be the top and bottom rails. Space the rails so the bottom rail will be 3 inches above the decking. Cut the spindles so they'll end flush with the rails. Lay out the width of the panel so the space between spindles is less than 4 inches, and make a spacer block to help keep the spindle spacing uniform. Screw one end of all the spindles to one of the rails, then screw down the other ends. You can make the panel design as complex as you like, with spindles on both sides of the rails, intermediate rails, and decorative blocks.

To install the panel, you'll probably have to tug the posts apart a bit, or perhaps push them together. This is because posts are rarely perfectly straight; installing this style of panel will help to pull the posts into line. Drill pilot holes and screw through the edge spindles into the posts.

Cap rail

With most styles of railing, the cap is a 2x6 tightly screwed to the posts. You can screw down through the cap into the posts, you can screw upward from underneath, or you can make the connection with a concealed metal clip.

When rail sections turn corners, you'll probably want to make a miter joint. One way to do this is to cut both pieces to the correct angle and fasten one of them in place. Bring the other one up to it and run the saw through the joint. This maneuver removes any inaccuracies, allowing you to butt the pieces tightly together. Fasten the pieces together with screws driven through the edge of one piece into the other.

1 *Assemble railing panels* flat. A temporary corner jig helps keep the panels square while you assemble them.

2 *Screw the assembled* railing panels to the posts. Predrill the spindles so they don't split.

3 *Align the cap rail* on top of the posts and screw it in place.

Stair Rails

Most building codes specify a handrail on any flight of four or more steps. The railing goes on the open side or on both sides, 34 to 38 inches above the front edge of the treads. The most direct way of installing the handrail is by screwing it to spindles fastened to the stringer. If the spindles are all the same length, they'll all end up at the same height relative to the treads, so they'll follow the slope of the stair.

Start by finding the slope of the stairs – this will determine the angle at which all the rail pieces are cut. To do this, temporarily clamp a 1x6 to the posts at the top and bottom of the stairs, and position it by measuring up the same distance from the top and bottom tread nosings. Then set a bevel gauge to the angle between the temporary rail and the post; use this angle to make the angle cuts for the rail and spindles. Finally, attach the real handrail and screw everything together.

Most people make the handrail out of the same material they used for the deck cap rail – typically, 2x6 lumber. However, in most areas code requires a graspable handrail, which means that either a groove has to be routed into the 2x6, or else a second, graspable handrail has to be attached.

1 *Mock up the stair rail by clamping a 1x6 to the posts. Make the temporary rail 36 inches above the front edge of the top and bottom treads. This establishes the slope of the rail.*

2 *Set a bevel gauge to the angle between the posts and the temporary railing. Use this angle to cut the tops of the spindles and the ends of the rail pieces.*

3 *Make a spacer block to help position the spindles, then screw them in place. The spacer works best if it is cut to the same angle as the other handrail parts.*

Graspable handrail

The building code may require you to install a graspable handrail on one side of the stair. This railing mounts on standard handrail brackets. The mitered end return makes a neat finish, though it probably will take some trial and error to get right. Drill pilot holes before you drive the screws. See page 25 for other graspable rail designs.

ADVANCED BUILDING TECHNIQUES

Different levels, angles, or curves can transform a deck into an out-of-the-ordinary living space and make it more pleasant to view and to use. Some techniques require more skill and know-how than others, but all are within the reach of a do-it-yourselfer willing to take the time to do a little extra work.

Since some of the techniques shown in this chapter require structural modifications to a deck, it is extremely important to work closely with your local building department in developing the design and the building plans.

Framing a Multi-Level Deck

A multi-level deck is just a series of simple decks joined together. In most situations, two adjacent platforms at different heights can share a support beam and posts. Exactly how the decks connect depends mostly on how much height difference you want.

If the height difference is small and the upper deck is also quite small, the simplest solution is to build the lower section to cover the entire area. Then build the upper platform right on top of the lower one, by framing a second set of joists directly on top of, and at right angles to, the first set.

Another option for a small height change is to rest the rim joist of the upper level directly on the rim joist of the lower platform. If the joist depth doesn't give you the elevation you want, you can insert 2x4 spacers between the rim joists.

For a greater difference in height, you can build a low stud wall between the two deck platforms instead of using a 2x4 spacer. This approach requires building the lower platform first, then erecting the wall on top of it, and finally building the upper platform with its rim joist resting on top of the low wall.

Another way of supporting two decks is with a row of shared posts. The beam or rim joist of the upper platform rests on the top of the posts, while the lower platform rests on a beam that is bolted into a notch cut into the face of the posts. This method allows you to build in stages if you like: first the upper platform, then the lower one a year or two later.

Shared posts support *the stacked rim joists of this two-level deck. The doubled rim joist of the upper level rests on a spacer of doubled 2x4s. (The spacer increases the height change between levels to 14 inches – perfect for a box step with a 7-inch rise.) The spacer rests on a beam made up of three 2x10s.*

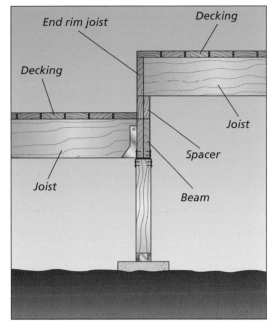

For a one-step difference in height, rest the rim joist of the upper deck directly on the rim joist of the lower one. Adjust the height with a spacer between the levels.

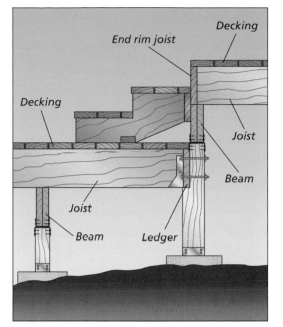

For a two- or three-step difference in height, insert a beam between the lower deck and the upper one. You can use a ledger to support the edge of the lower deck, or you can rest it directly on the post.

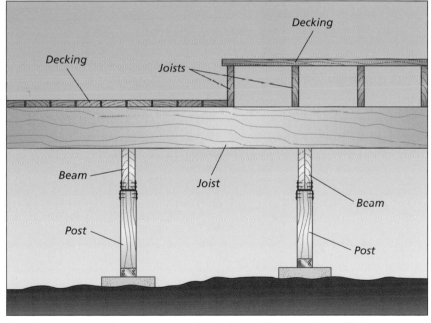

Another way to make a one-step variation is to add a second set of joists on top of the lower deck. The upper joists are perpendicular to the lower ones.

Change levels with a box step

A box step is a good way to connect two decks at different heights. Make the step the full width of the overlap between decks. People will use it for seating as well as for moving from one level to the other. Frame up a simple box with rim joists and field joists, then toenail it to the deck. To make the tread, attach deck boards to the joists.

Framing for a Spa

When choosing a spot for a spa, avoid overhead wires and windy areas. Also check your local building code for possible restrictions and obtain any necessary permits. Spas filled with water are extremely heavy and must be supported adequately. On raised decks, you should consult a structural engineer to make sure that you have the necessary support.

An above-deck spa must be supported by double rim joists and possibly extra beams and posts. Here the joists are spaced 12 inches on center, the ledger has been doubled, and extra posts have been installed.

Spas may either be installed above the deck or be inset into the deck. The deck understructure for above-deck spas must be modified to make sure the deck will be able to support the maximum load of the water-filled spa. In an inset installation, the body of the spa is positioned below the deck but is mounted so that the upper portion rises above the deck boards. It's best to leave space for an inset spa during initial construction, but if necessary you can go back and adapt an existing deck to accept a spa. You'll have to remove enough deck boards to create the rough opening, and add under-deck framing to support the weight. Save any wood you re-

move, because you can reuse it in the framing later on.

Purchase your spa before beginning any work on the deck. This way you'll have the exact weight and measurements, which will let you properly size the rough opening and frame the support system. Once the spa is in position and leveled, you can install nailers and scribe the deck boards to fit neatly around it. Make sure the decking doesn't block off access to the spa's control panel.

1 *To frame a rough opening* for an inset spa, you'll have to remove the decking and cut through the joists underneath the deck. Then add new beams and doubled joists directly under the spa.

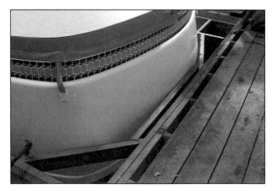

2 *Install blocking* close to the shape of the spa, so you can nail deck boards right up to it.

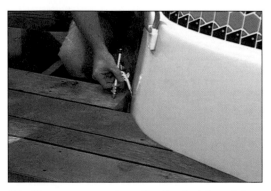

3 *Use a compass* to scribe the deck boards to the contour of the spa. Leave clearance of about ¼ inch.

Framing around Trees

Trees and other landscape features can be framed with an inset. To create an inset, you simply box out an opening that allows the tree or other feature to come through. Because the inset will interrupt the span of one or more joists, you must fortify the framework with double joists on each side of the inset, and with a header at each end. In some situations you could need an additional post as well.

Make sure the opening will accommodate the tree as it grows. Leave a minimum of 12 inches on all sides of a young tree.

Installing the decking

To support the decking within the inset frame, you will need to install nailing blocks between the joists and headers. Make sure the ends of the decking boards do not extend more than 4 inches unsupported beyond the nailing blocks. If you install short deck boards within the inset frame, you can trim them quite close to the tree trunk. However, as the tree grows, you will have to trim them back or replace them in a couple of years. Don't allow the deck boards to chafe the trunk of the tree, or the tree could die.

A beautiful tree can enhance a deck and vice versa. Just make sure to leave enough space between the tree trunk and the framing to allow the tree to grow.

1 *Box out the open area* for the tree with a header capping the ends of the interrupted joists.

2 *Add blocking* to nail the decking onto the joists and the headers.

Picture-Frame Decking

There are many ways to lay decking – perpendicular to the joists, diagonal to the joists, or in a herringbone design, to name just a few. Another popular style is picture-frame decking. In picture-frame decking the ends of the deck boards are enclosed by a border made from pieces of 2x8 lumber. The ends of the 2x8s can be mitered for a finished look, but they don't have to be.

Double joists

It doesn't take any complicated carpentry to create a picture-frame decking pattern. While many other patterns require complex modifications to the understructure to support the decking, a single-board picture frame requires only one change: adding a double joist about three inches away from each side rim joist. The double joist supports both the 2x8 border pieces and the ends of the deck boards. (Wider frames will need more support, as shown on page 23.)

To install a double joist that is close to the rim joist, put double joist hangers on the ends before installing it. This way, when you put it in place, you won't have to swing the hammer side-to-side to nail into the joists. You'll only have to swing along the length of the joist to drive nails through the hanger into the ledger and end rim joist.

Installing the frame

Start with the long piece that goes across the outside end of the deck. This piece has 45-degree miters on both ends. Screw it down to the field joists and to the rim joists. Then put in the side pieces. These are square on one end and mitered on the other.

Keep the boards parallel

Start installing the decking at the outside edge of the deck, and work back toward the house. To achieve a consistent gap between the ends of the deck boards and the sides of the picture frame, cut each piece to length as carefully as possible. As you get closer to the house, make sure to frequently double-check that the boards will be parallel to the house. If they're just a little bit off, it won't be noticeable until you're right next to the house – and then it will be too late to do anything about it. Catching errors early on will allow you to make undetectable adjustments in the gaps between the boards.

Straight cuts

Because you can't trim the deck boards to length after they're installed (as you can with decking that runs out to the rim joists), each deck board must be cut to exact length before it's installed. The board ends also have to be perfectly square. To cut them, either use a power miter saw or use a speed square to guide a circular saw while cutting.

Install a doubled joist next to each side rim joist. This will provide a nailing surface for the picture frame boards and for the ends of the decking boards.

A mitered corner is the neatest joint to use in picture frame construction. You can also butt the frame pieces, but you will see end grain on whichever piece runs long.

Predrill the screw holes near the ends of the deck boards so the wood won't split when you fasten them to the joists below. If a second drill isn't available, a drill-drive bit will speed up the process.

Cutaway Corners

The simplest way to visualize and design an angled deck is to picture a square or rectangular deck with one or more corners lopped off. When designing the layout, it may be tempting to use irregular angles, but they are much harder to measure and cut accurately. It's a good idea to limit yourself to 45-degree angles. This will make the joists easier to cut and will also make the joists easier to install, since 45-degree joist hangers are readily available at home centers.

To make sure the joists end up the right length, install them long, then snap a chalk line across the corner, transfer the marks down the sides of the joists, and trim them

Mark the angled cut along the joists by snapping a chalk line across the corner. Nail a section of rim joist to the ends of the angled joists. It should be mitered where it joins the doubled side rim joist.

to length. If you are using 45-degree joist hangers, you can trim the joist ends flush. Otherwise, set the circular saw to cut at a 45-degree angle so the joists ends will sit flush against the rim joist.

Nail the mitered ends of the straight rim section to the angled sections. There can't be any free joist ends – they all have to be fastened to a rim joist.

Screw the decking to the joists, then snap a chalk line and trim the deck boards.

Build in some angles to give a plain deck a visual boost or to make the deck flow with the landscape. This is easiest to do when the joists are cantilevered over the beam.

Curves

A section of curved decking can turn a plain deck into an eye-catcher. Curves can also ease the transition from the rectangular shape of the house to the rounded shapes of the landscape.

When building curves into your deck, expect scrutiny from the building inspector. This is because most curved decks use cantilevered construction, where the decking hangs over a beam that is set back from the edge of the deck. Make sure your plans are accurate and that you enclose a complete list of building materials.

The simplest way to make a gentle curve is to let the decking run long over a straight end rim joist. Then cut the overhanging deck boards into a curved shape.

If you prefer to make a curved rim joist, one way is to saw closely spaced cuts, called kerfs or relief cuts, into the back of the rim joists. These cuts don't quite go all the way through the wood. The kerfed wood will bend though it does not have much strength, so you'll need to install straight blocking as close to the curved rim joist as possible. Another way is to glue and clamp six layers of ¼-inch exterior plywood together. The plywood is thin enough to follow the curved shape. A bent plywood joist is very strong. Curved handrails can be made in the same way, using thin plywood or thin strips of solid wood.

Draw an arc using a tape measure fastened with a small nail at the center point of the curve, then transfer the marks down the sides of the joists. Cut the angled joist ends with a handsaw or a reciprocating saw.

A curved rim joist allows the deck to follow these graceful shapes. Make the rim joist with a kerfed board shimmed and nailed to the joist ends.

SPECIAL FEATURES

Built-in planters, benches, privacy screens, sunshades, and trellises all increase the usability of the deck. They also give the deck a custom look and make the space uniquely your own. Bonus: While these features add a lot of visual pizzazz, most of them are easy and quick to build.

And don't forget about lighting. The proper lighting can make your deck as pleasant to use by night as by day. Low-voltage lights are the backbone of many lighting schemes, but floods, spotlights, and wall-mounted outdoor lamps all have roles to play in creating an attractive nightscape.

Benches, Planters, and Deck Skirts

In addition to providing seating, benches can help divide a deck into separate areas and give it a more finished look. Benches can be either freestanding or built into a section of railing. Depending on the design and local code requirements, a built-in bench can even substitute for a railing. On low decks that don't require a railing by code (usually decks 30 inches or lower off the ground), benches can act as barriers, defining the edge of the deck and protecting people from an accidental tumble.

Typical bench height ranges from 15 to 18 inches. Typical seat depth is at least 15 inches, although benches without backs can be as deep as 30 inches. Benches with backs will be more comfortable if you slant the backs slightly (no more than 10 degrees). On any bench, make sure to round off all sharp edges and corners with a hand plane or a Surform rasp. Like any feature you add to the deck, benches look best if they match the material used for the decking and railing.

Planters

Planters don't need to be complicated. They may be as simple as a wooden box with feet or wheels (either will allow air circulation underneath). One good way to make planters is to nail decking scraps to 4x4 posts; this way, you get to use up all your scraps. If you're not using decking remnants, choose rot-resistant wood such as cedar, redwood, or pressure-treated lumber for your planters.

Before you build a planter, decide what kind of plants you'll be growing in it. Planters that will contain shrubs should be between 18 and 24 inches deep, but those for annuals and perennials can be much shallower (8 to 10 inches). On shady decks, freestanding planters are especially useful because you can lug (or roll) sun-loving plants around as necessary to catch the sunshine they need.

Plants can either be planted directly in the planter or potted up and placed in the planter. For direct planting, you'll need to line the planter with a sheet of plastic before you add the soil. Poke a drainage hole in the bottom so moisture can escape; this will prevent the roots from becoming soggy and rotting.

Overlap the 2x2 seat-decking pieces where they meet and you'll get a nice herringbone effect without having to fit a lot of miters. The 2x2s are spaced about ½ inch apart for drainage. The seat rail at the front is a 2x4 set on edge.

Strength equals safety when building deck benches. A 2x4 brace on each side supports this bench; a straight 2x4 props up the seat at the center. Fasten the bench parts together with 3-inch galvanized or resin-coated screws.

Deck skirts

Low decks may need no skirting between the deck boards and the ground, but some sort of skirting is often installed on raised decks to enclose the storage space underneath. Because the panels are inexpensive and easy to install, lattice is by far the most popular material for deck skirts. Lattice panels are available in pressure-treated wood, redwood, and cedar. Don't let any deck skirt rest directly on the ground or it will eventually rot.

Lattice panels come in various weights depending on the size of the grid. The more lightweight the lattice, the more flexible, and the trickier it will be to cut to size. It's easiest to cut lattice if you sandwich it between two pieces of plywood, and saw through the whole sandwich.

Lattice bends easily, so it's best to attach the panels to a frame; this provides support and protects the edges. Channel molding makes a good frame, as long as the width of the channel equals the thickness of the lattice, but a nailed-together wood frame with lattice fastened to it works just as well. Hinge one of the frames to the deck posts, so you can get into the storage space.

Build planters *with scraps left over from the deck. Here, pieces of 2x6 connect to the top and bottom frames, which are made from 2x2s. If you need to rip the last 2x6 to fit, place the cut edge toward the center of the planter and the smooth factory edge on the corner.*

Lattice panels *make excellent deck skirts because they allow air circulation yet hide the structure of the deck. Lattice comes in 4x8 sections, which you can cut to size. Nail it up so it doesn't rest directly on the ground.*

Lighting

The way you intend to use your deck will influence the amount and type of lighting you install. If your deck is used primarily as a daytime play space for children, for example, you will have different lighting needs than if you like to entertain under the stars. Even decks that receive little or no nighttime use should incorporate some type of lighting into their design. At the very least, well-lit stairs are a necessity for safe passage after dark.

Low-voltage lighting is a good overall choice because it's inexpensive and you can install it yourself. No permit is necessary. The soft light is just strong enough to highlight the deck so you'll be able to appreciate it both from inside and out. Since low-voltage systems are powered by a transformer that's plugged into a standard outlet, first make sure that the transformer can handle all the lights on the deck. Count all the lights, add up the wattage, and compare the total to the capacity of the transformer.

You can supplement and accent low-voltage lighting with a variety of spotlights, floodlights, and wall-mounted outdoor lights. In general, keep strong lights out of the field of vision of deck occupants so you don't blind them. For a dramatic effect, position an up-light at the base of a tree, so that the light plays through its branches. Depending on local code requirements, lights other than low-voltage types may require a permit and professional installation. Check with your building department to find out what's needed and at what points during construction the electrical installation should be inspected.

1 **To hide the wires** for post-mounted low-voltage lighting, you'll need to create a recess in the post. Drill out as much waste as possible, then clean up with a chisel.

2 **Staple** low-voltage cable where it will be the least obvious, in this case, along the back side of the railing. The cable comes through the post at the first lighting position then continues down the line to the next light.

3 **Connect the fixture wires** to the cable with wire connectors, then tuck all the wires into the recess and screw the light to the post.

4 **Set the timer** so the lights go on and off when you want. Units with both a timer and a daylight sensor are handy because the sensor turns the lights on at dusk, and the timer turns them off whenever you specify.

Privacy Screens

With the addition of a privacy screen along one or two sides, a deck can become a quiet retreat in any neighborhood. What's more, depending on where it's located, a privacy screen can cast some welcome shade on hot afternoons. Planting vines in pots at the base of the screen will give you flowers and foliage to enjoy throughout the growing season.

Privacy screens are usually made using the same design, materials, and construction techniques as the deck railing, only they're built higher. One benefit to doing it this way is that all the visible parts of the deck work together to create a unified look. Another benefit is that you don't need to learn any new construction techniques.

If you're feeling adventurous, you can design a privacy screen using a variety of materials and techniques, from redwood basket weave fencing and translucent acrylic panels to the ever-popular lattice. Most of these materials have to be retained by a rigid supporting frame, but the frame doesn't have to be complex. Four pieces of wood butted or mitered at the ends will work fine.

Use the perimeter deck posts or tall railing posts to support the privacy screen, the same way they support the deck railing. Build the screen flat on the deck, then position it and screw it to the posts. Make sure the posts are solidly attached to the deck and that the screen is securely to attached to the posts. It's a good idea to beef up these connections in areas prone to high winds.

1 *To notch the posts* for the screen rails, mark the ends of the notch, then score the area between them with closely spaced cuts. Knock out the scrap with a hammer, then clean up the notch with a chisel and check the fit with a scrap of rail material.

2 *Square up* the frame by measuring the diagonals with a tape measure; both measurements should be the same. If they're not, adjust the frame.

3 *Test-fit the frame* into the posts, adjust as necessary, then lay the frame on the deck to attach all the spindles.

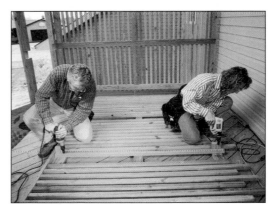

4 *Screw the spindles* to the rails using spacer blocks to maintain even spacing between them. When the panel is complete, drill pilot holes and screw the frame to the posts.

Overhead Structures

An overhead structure is an extension of your indoor living space. It adds architectural interest to your deck while providing shelter. In all designs, it's important to consider the seasonal changes in the path of the sun so you'll get shade when it's most needed without blocking morning or evening sun. You can control the amount of sunlight that will penetrate the structure by varying the size and spacing of the framing components. One good way to size up your situation is to install some temporary slats and watch how they interact with the patterns of the sun.

Build an overhead structure the same way you built the deck itself: posts hold it up, rails tie the posts together just like a rim joist, rafters fill in between the rails. Since the overhead structure won't be decked over and doesn't have to carry any load beyond its own weight, it can be made of lighter material. However, be sure to screw it together securely, so it doesn't blow away.

While you could construct the overhead structure by teetering on ladders, it's easier to build it flat on the deck, then lift it into place. To support a large structure while you screw it in position, use 2x4s as temporary posts.

3 *Lay the overhead lattice* on the rafters and nail it in place. Then trim out the edges with 1x2 molding.

1 *Define the perimeter* of the overhead structure by fitting 2x6 rails around the posts. Screw the rails to the posts.

2 *Cut, fit, and fasten rafters* between the rails. Space the rafters 16 inches apart, same as for the deck joists.

4 *To block* the hot afternoon sun, this overhead also has lattice attached to the side. After the deck is finished check all the bolts to make sure they haven't loosened during construction.

FINISHES

Finishing your deck is all about protecting your investment *and there's no solid wood that doesn't need some protection. Even cedar, redwood, and pressure-treated decking aren't maintenance-free. If you do nothing, these woods will still look attractive as they weather to a go-with-everything gray, but they could become dry and splintery and more likely to warp, crack, and mildew. Even if you don't want to change the color of the wood with a stain, you should consider a water repellent specially formulated for decks. This will protect the wood from moisture-related damage and help keep your deck looking new.*

Finish gallery. *Here's a comparison of common deck finishes on pressure-treated wood (top in each pair) and on redwood.*

Opaque gray stain: *An opaque stain is a lot like paint. It covers most of the color of the wood, without forming a thick coating on the surface. Nevertheless, opaque stains are liable to peel in the weather and must be renewed regularly.*

Semi-transparent gray stain: *Stains contain the same ingredients as clear finishes, with the addition of pigment that's designed to let the color and texture of the wood show through. A stain is the best way to disguise the green hue of pressure-treated wood.*

Water repellent: *A water repellent has the least effect on the color of the wood, but by keeping water from penetrating the wood, it does the most good. Water repellents should be renewed every year or two.*

Clear finish: *This penetrating coating intensifies the natural color of the wood, and it makes the pressure-treated sample dark. If the coating doesn't contain UV inhibitors, sunlight will soon break it down.*

Finish Choices

There's a confusing array of deck-finishing products available, but most choices boil down to some combination of sealer, preservative, and stain. Paint isn't recommended for wood decks because it peels and shows wear along traffic paths. All formulations differ by manufacturer, so read labels carefully to know exactly what you're buying and how often you'll need to reapply it.

Deck sealers, often called water repellents, penetrate the wood and help it shed water, which reduces swelling, shrinking, and warping. Some decking is available with a water repellent embedded right in the wood, so no further finishing is needed. Deck sealers contain lots of wax, which causes rainwater to bead up. Some also contain mildewcides, and others have semi-transparent colorants, which can cut the green cast of pressure-treated wood.

Clear wood preservatives are similar to deck sealers except they typically contain less wax so water beading is less obvious. Most preservatives include fungicides to control mildew growth on shady areas.

Stains will change the color of the wood. They're useful if you want to match parts of the deck to the house or trim color. Stains can be semi-transparent or opaque, and while semi-transparent types penetrate the wood better, they're not always available in the colors you want. A good compromise is to buy opaque stain, and thin it with blending base (available at home centers) before application. If your deck receives a lot of foot traffic, seal the wood but don't put any type of stain on the decking boards. Foot traffic will quickly erode the stain, leaving a mottled surface behind.

Wood-composite decking

Decking made from a combination of recycled plastic and wood products can be finished just like solid wood, though more for cosmetic reasons than for protection. Since wood-composite material fades to silvery gray from its initial light brown over a period of about 3 months, manufacturers suggest that you wait to apply semi-transparent stain until fading is complete.

How dry is dry?

Some experts recommend that wood should season for several months before being finished because premature finishing will trap moisture and cause peeling and blistering as the water evaporates. Others maintain that allowing wood to go this long without some sort of finish is an invitation to surface damage and can substantially reduce the effectiveness of whatever finish you eventually apply. To sidestep this debate, finish your deck immediately with a product formulated for new wood, or use a breathable penetrating finish. If the wood is wet, you should still wait a week or two before finishing. How do you tell if the wood is wet? Sprinkle on some water. If the water soaks in, the wood is dry enough to be finished.

Applying deck finishes

More is not better when applying deck finishes. One coat is plenty when applied properly, and too thick an application actually can prevent proper penetration of the finish and cause a sticky mess that never quite dries. For the best job, make sure the deck is clean, dry, and free of dust and dirt.

The quickest way to apply a finish is by spraying. Spraying is especially effective for coating irregular or intricate shapes like trellises, complex railings, and privacy screens. Spraying gives a more even finish than a brush or roller. Be sure to pick a windless day for spraying. You can use a garden sprayer,

an airless paint sprayer, or a paint sprayer powered by an air compressor. Most manufacturers recommend that the finish be back-brushed after spraying to ensure deep penetration and to eliminate drips and runs. While back-brushing, work the finish into tight areas and cracks where the spray didn't reach.

When rolling a finish on deck boards, use a short-nap lambswool roller on an extension pole. Make sure you always keep a wet edge to avoid lap marks. A soft, synthetic-bristle broom is a good tool to push deck finish into the gaps between widely spaced boards.

No matter what method you use, make sure all end-grain surfaces – tops of posts and balusters and ends of deck boards – are completely coated with finish. End grain is really absorbent so more finish may be required than on other surfaces.

Spray on stain *using a pump sprayer, then back-brush it to catch drips and to help work the stain deeper into the pores of the wood.*

Rolling on clear finishes *with a roller and extension handle is the way to cover lots of ground quickly. Overlap wet areas by about ½ inch to avoid lap marks.*

For a weathered look *without the wait, finish your deck with either a gray stain or a bleaching oil. Bleaching oil works with the power of sun and water, so it's necessary to wet down the deck occasionally to hasten weathering.*

Renewing Wood

Blistering, peeling, or deteriorating deck finishes may have to be stripped before a new coat of finish can be applied. If you're not sure what type of finish is on the deck, use a commercial deck stripper formulated to remove both oil and latex finishes. A gel-type deck stripper is easiest to use because it clings to vertical surfaces (such as railing posts and spindles).

If the deck finish is basically sound, but just discolored or stained with mildew, you can probably get by with a deck brightener instead of a stripper. Deck brighteners, which usually are based on oxygen bleach, work by lifting and loosening ground-in dirt and removing the uppermost layer of sun-damaged wood fibers. They can restore even weathered decks to their former appeal. Make sure that the product you buy is safe to use around plants and shrubs.

Chlorine bleach, or household bleach, is best limited to spot-cleaning stubborn stains left by mildew, leaves, algae, and moss. Use a 1:1 solution of household bleach and water, and scrub vigorously. After bleaching, thoroughly rinse the wood before applying a finishing product. Don't substitute bleach for a deck brightener, since bleach isn't as effective at cleaning ground-in dirt or removing weathered wood fibers. Plus it can turn the wood unnaturally white.

The tannins in redwood may react with fasteners, causing black stains on the wood. These stains can be removed with an oxalic-acid based bleach, followed by washing with a regular deck cleaner to remove dirt and mildew.

1 *Clean out* decayed leaves, twigs, and other debris from the gaps between deck boards with a putty knife. Anything stuck between the boards will trap moisture and encourage rot.

2 *Apply deck brightener* with a garden sprayer. Complete work on a 4-foot band across the deck before moving on to the next band. You can also brush, mop, or roll the solution onto the wood.

3 *Wait three to five minutes* for the deck brightener to sink in and do its work, then brush the decking with a stiff brush to remove the top layer of damaged wood fibers.

4 *Rinse off the deck brightener* with water from a garden hose or a power washer. Let the deck dry completely before applying new finish.

Index